Fossil Elephantoids

From the Hominid-Bearing Awash Group, Middle Awash Valley, Afar Depression, Ethiopia

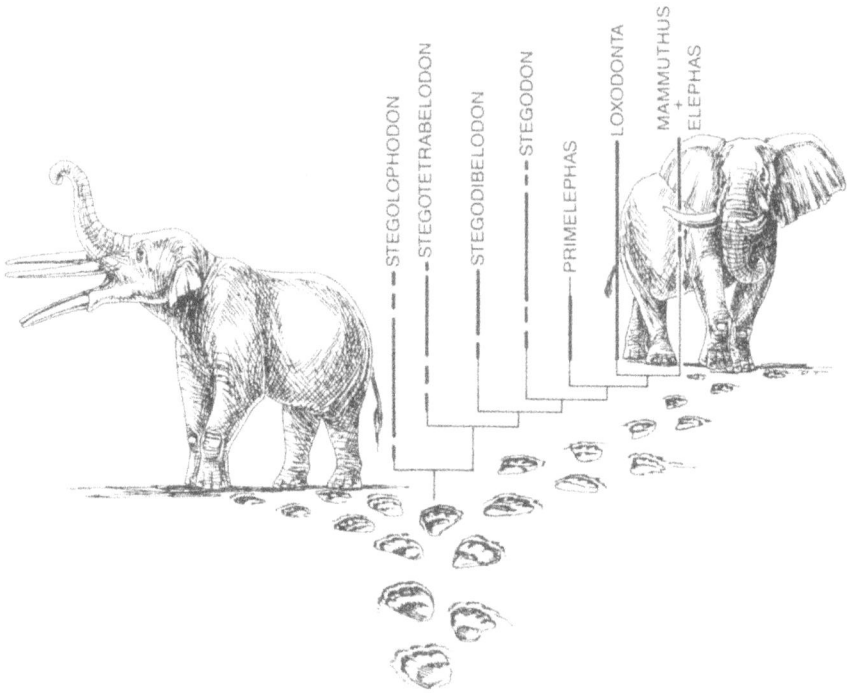

FRONTISPIECE. Phylogeny of the Elephantidae.

TRANSACTIONS

of the

American Philosophical Society

Held at Philadelphia for Promoting Useful Knowledge

VOLUME 83, Part 1, 1993

Fossil Elephantoids
From the
Hominid-Bearing Awash Group, Middle Awash Valley, Afar Depression, Ethiopia

JON E. KALB
ASSEFA MEBRATE

Proboscidean drawings by DORIS TISCHLER

THE AMERICAN PHILOSOPHICAL SOCIETY

Independence Square, Philadelphia

1993

Library of Congress Catalog
Card Number: 92-82797
International Standard Book Number 0-87169-831-5
US ISSN 0065-9746

TABLE OF CONTENTS

PREFACE

From 1975–1978, the Rift Valley Research Mission in Ethiopia (RVRME) led by one of us (JK) recovered the most diverse collection of elephantoids known from a single area, from the Middle Awash Valley in the southwestern Afar Depression. These fossils come from the one-kilometer thick Awash Group, which has also yielded abundant numbers of early hominids, particularly those from the middle Pliocene site of Hadar referred to as *Australopithecus afarensis*.

Initial surveys by the RVRME in 1975 showed that extensive fossiliferous deposits are present in the Middle Awash area bearing elephantoid fossils far more primitive than those at Hadar, clearly extending the fossil record in the region to the base of the Pliocene and into the upper Miocene. In addition, these same surveys, and those conducted throughout 1976, also revealed extensive post-Hadar fossiliferous sediments. These deposits were shown to be of upper Pliocene and Pleistocene age, as indicated by successively more progressive elephantine taxa. Together these finds indicated that the Hadar hominid sequence is bracketed above and below by thick successions of deposits containing vertebrate fossils. Thus, as biostratigraphic indicators, the elephantoid fossils alone made it apparent that the Middle Awash would likely yield the ancestors as well as the successors of the Hadar hominids. In this regard, the RVRME discovered hundreds of post-Hadar archeological occurrences, some associated with elephant remains, one of which produced a largely complete cranium of archaic *Homo*. In 1982, after the RVRME ceased operations for political reasons, surveys in sites discovered by the RVRME yielded hominid fossils nearly a million years older than the well-known "Lucy" skeleton.

In this report, we describe in detail the elephantoids from the Middle Awash region, from the pre-Hadar Adu-Asa and Sagantole formations to the post-Hadar Matabaietu and Wehaietu formations. We also report briefly on the fossil elephants from the Hadar Formation itself and note elephantoids collected from deposits north of Hadar and south of the Middle Awash (the Chorora region).

The overall Awash sequence contains no fewer than 16 distinct taxa from the superfamily Elephantoidea. Of these, those from the Adu-Asa and Sagantole formations consist of two species of *Anancus*, one of tetralophodont type and the other pentalophodont, and all known genera of the family Elephantidae (as it is presently defined), except *Stegolophodon*. These taxa consist of *Stegotetrabelodon*, *Stegodibelodon*, *Stegodon*, and the subfamily Elephantinae, *Primelephas*, *Loxodonta*, *Mammuthus* and *Elephas*. The Hadar Formation itself is noted only for the elephantines, *Elephas*,

Loxodonta, and reportedly a new species of *Mammuthus.* Derived forms of *Loxodonta* and *Elephas* are present in the Matabaietu Formation, and only very progressive *Elephas recki* is confirmed thus far from the Wehaietu Formation.

Concerning the phylogeny of the elephantoids, we describe the relationships of the Awash *Anancus* to other *Anancus* in Africa, and to other late surviving "gomphotheres." We give additional evidence supporting the sister group relationship of the brevirostrine gomphotheres (*Anancus*) to the Elephantidae. Also, we describe new relationships of the African elephantids—the sister group of the genus *Stegolophodon*—to one another, as they relate to the Middle Awash fossils. Lastly, we reexamine the status of the Elephantinae—the sister group of the genus *Stegodon*—and suggest that a taxonomic reevaluation of the subfamily may be in order.

JON E. KALB
Vertebrate Paleontology Laboratory
Balcones Research Center
University of Texas
Austin, Texas 78712, USA

ASSEFA MEBRATE
Ethiopian Commission for Science and Technology
P. O. Box 2490
Addis Ababa, Ethiopia

LIST OF FIGURES

Frontispiece: Phylogeny of the Elephantidae (based on Figs. 6 and 41, also Maglio, 1973, Frontispiece). *Stegotetrabelodon*, the earliest confirmed African elephantid (left side), shown with the living African elephant (right side), *Loxodonta africana*. Drawn by D. Tischler.

(Section 3, A–A', Figs. 4 & 5, Kalb et al. 1982c). **2. Asa Koma** (Site 2, Fig. 2) (Section 5, A–A', Figs. 4 & 5, Kalb et al. 1982c). **3. Adu Dora North** (Site 1, Fig. 2) (Sections 7 & 8, A–A', Figs. 4 & 5, Kalb et al. 1982c). **4. Amba-Kuseralee** (Sites 6 & 7, Fig. 2) (Section 12, A–A', Figs. 4 & 5, Kalb et al. 1982c). **5. Haradaso to Beearyada** (between Sites 8 & 9, Fig. 2) (composite of Sections 16–23, A–A', Figs. 4 & 5, Kalb et al. 1982c). **6. Wee-ee to Hargufia** (between Sites 12–16, Fig. 2) (composite of: Fig. 2 in Hall et al. 1984; Sections 24–26, B–B' and Section 65, C–C', Figs. 4 & 5, Kalb et al. 1982c; approximate positions of intercalated basalts from Wee-ee section, Fig. 2 of Haileab and Brown 1992 and from Sections 65 & 68, C–C', Figs. 4 & 5 of Kalb et al. 1982c). **7. Asaberi** (between Sites 11 & 12, Fig. 2) (from Fig. 2, Haileab and Brown, 1992). **8. Kalaloo-Bodo** (between Sites 15 & 16, Fig. 2) (sequence below Cindery Tuff (CT) from: Section 5, Fig. 2, Hall et al. 1984; and Section 24, B–B', Figs. 4 & 5, Kalb et al. 1982c). **9. Bodo** (between Sites 15 & 16, Fig. 2) (sequence above CT from: Sections 25 & 26, B–B', Figs. 4 & 5, Kalb et al. 1982c; and Section BOD-G 13, Fig. 6, Williams et al. 1986). **10. Amado** (NW of Hadar, Fig. 1) (from Kalb, in press). Amado Tuffs indicated at AMT-1 and -2 (see column 10 on Fig. 5).

5. Stratigraphy of the Awash Group: the Hadar, Matabaietu and Wehaietu formations.

Continuation of Fig. 4; see text for abbreviations ("Location and Stratigraphy"). Legend to location of sites and numbered sections: **10. Amado** (NW of Hadar, Fig. 1) (from Kalb, in press). Amado Tuffs indicated as AMT-1 and -2. **11. Gona** (NW of Site 22, Fig. 2) (Pl. 2, Taieb et al. 1978; Roche and Tiercelin 1980). **12. Dakanihyalo** (SW margin of Hatowie Graben, Fig. 2) (Section 57, C–C', Figs. 3–5, Kalb et al. 1982c). **13. Buri** (SW margin of Hatowie Graben, Fig. 2) (Section 56, C–C', Figs. 3–5, Kalb et al. 1982c). **14. Denen Dora—Kada Damoumou Koma** (between Sites 22 & 23, Fig. 2) (from: Fig. 1, Aronson et al. 1977; Pl. 2, Taieb et al. 1978; Sections 41–47, B–B', Figs. 4–5, Kalb et al. 1982c). **15. Wilti Dora** (Site 14, Fig. 2) (see p. 107 & Fig. 3, Kalb et al. 1982c). **16. Matabaietu** (Site 13, Fig. 2) (Sections 71–73, C–C', Figs. 4 & 5 and p. 107, Kalb et al. 1982c). **17. Bodo** (between Sites 15 & 16, Fig. 2) (Section 28, B–B', Figs. 4 & 5, Kalb et al. 1982c; also, Kalb et al. 1980). **18. Subalealo** (Site 19, Fig. 2) (Section 35, B–B', Figs. 4 & 5, Kalb et al. 1982c). **19. Geraru** (Fig. 1). Symbols refer to Data Koma Tuffs (DKT) and basalt (DKB) and Geraru Tuffs (GR-1, -2, -3) (from Kalb, in press). **20. Geraru.** Upper section, including the Upper Geraru Tuffs (UGT) (Kalb, in press). **21. Meadura** (Site 17, Fig. 2) (Section 30, B–B', Figs. 4 & 5, Kalb et al. 1982c). **22. Andalee** (Site 21, Fig. 2) (Kalb et al. 1982a; Sections 34 & 37, C–C', Figs. 4 & 5, Kalb et al. 1982c).

6. Summary stratigraphy, radiometric dates and distribution of proboscideans in the Awash Group.

7. Cladogram of late Neogene Proboscidea (from Kalb et al. 1992a).

8. Nomenclature for *Anancus* molars. Schematic figure is a right M^2 of a tetralophodont *Anancus* (occlusal view).

9. Nomenclature for elephantid molars. Schematic figure is a left M_2 of *Elephas recki* (occlusal view).

10. Schematic figures of tetralophodont and pentalophodont *Anancus* molars. All figures drawn to scale.

rM^2: **A.** Four lophs; modest talon; minimal wear; single posterior posttrite and pretrite (?) conules to end of molar. L222-1 (Fig. 16) from **Haradaso Member, Sagantole D'ar**; compares with L90-1 (Asa Member), L206-12 (Kuseralee Member), L224-1 (Haradaso Member) (Table 1). **B.** Four lophs; strong talon; very worn molar; no preserved conules, but single posterior posttrite and pretrite conules the length of the molar were probably present on unworn molar, as were double posterior posttrite conules anteriorly; holotype of *A. kenyensis* from **Kanam East** (MacInnes 1942, Pl. VII-5); KE 20 (reversed drawing in Fig. 10B) may be same individual as Fig. 10G and 10K). **C.** Four lophs; strong talon; moderate wear; single, double and triple posterior posttrite conules; single posterior pretrite conules; cement in valleys. PQ L-40012 from **Pelletal Phosphorite and Quartzose Sand Members undifferentiated (QSM/PPM), Varswater Formation, "E" Quarry, Langebaanweg**; compares with PQ L-41692 (QSM/PPM). **D.** Five lophs; small talon; moderate wear; single and triple posterior posttrite conules and single pretrite conules to end of molar; ectoflexus; cement. L227-1 (Fig. 19) from **upper Sagantole Formation, Beearyada** (Table 1). rM^3: **E.** Five lophs; small talon; moderate wear; single posterior posttrite and pretrite conules to mid-molar. KNM LU-57 from **Lukeino-A** (Tassy 1986, Pl. XIII-1a). **F.** Five lophs; small talon; moderate wear; single posterior posttrite and pretrite conules to mid-molar. L206-11 from **Kuseralee Member, Gulubahsin Dora**; compares with L323-1 from the Haradaso Member (Table 1). **G.** *Estimated* six lophs on complete molar; no wear posteriorally; small talon; *estimated* single, perhaps one or two double posterior posttrite conules to mid-molar and posterior pretrite conules to end of molar. Paratype of *A. kenyensis* from **Kanam East** (MacInnes 1942, Pl. VII-6); KE-24 (reversed drawing in Fig. 10), may be same individual as Figs. 10B and 10K. **H.** Six lophs; modest talon; slight wear; single and double posterior posttrite conules to mid-molar; single posterior pretrite conules anteriorly; single anterior pretrite conules to mid-molar; ectoflexus. KNM-BC 33 (reversed drawing in Fig. 10H) from **lower Chemeron Formation. I.** Six lophs; strong talon; no wear; single, double and triple posterior posttrite conules to mid-molar; single posterior and anterior conules to mid-molar; ectoflexus. PQ-L41692 from **PPM/QSM, Varswater Formation, "E" Quarry, Langebaanweg**; consistent with PQ-L2557 (Hendey 1970b, Pl. 3-A, 1982, 39), PQ-L4007, PQ-L5500, PQ-L2561, PQ-L4008 from PPM/QSM although specimens vary in number of conules and cement development—attributable to individual, environmental and modest stratigraphic differences. **J.** Seven lophs; small talon; heavy anterior wear; single, double and triple posterior posttrite conules to mid-molar; posterior pretrite conule anteriorly (matrix may obscure more conules); ectoflexus; cement. L337-3 (Fig. 17) (reversed drawing in Fig. 10J) from **upper Sagantole Formation, Bodo D'ar** (Table 1). rM_2: **K.** Four lophids; strong talonid; very worn molar; no preserved conules, but single posterior posttrite and pretrite conules to mid-molar were probably present on unworn molar. Specimen KE 21 (reversed drawing in Fig. 10K) (may be same individual as Fig. 10B and 10G) of *A. kenyensis* from **Kanam East** (MacInnes 1942, Pl. VII-4). **L.** Four lophids; strong talonid; well worn molar; single posterior posttrite and double pretrite conules to end of molar; cement. L1179 (reversed drawing in Fig. 10L) from **Lower Beds, Baard's Quarry, Langebaanweg** (Hendey 1978, Fig. 1). **M.** Five lophids; small talonid; single posterior posttrite and pretrite(?) conules to end of molar. No specimen number; from **Sahabi** (Petrocchi 1954, Pl. XII-B, poorly figured). **N.** Five lophids; modest talonid; slightly worn molar; single and double posterior posttrite and pretrite conules to end of molar; single anterior posttrite and pretrite conules; ectoflexus. KNM KP 384 (= "24-65K") (reversed drawing in Fig. 10N) from **Kanapoi** beds (Coppens et al. 1978, Fig. 17.4-B; Tassy 1986, Pl. XIII-3). rM_3: **O.** Five lophids (*six lophids on associated specimens*); modest talonid; moderate wear; single posterior posttrite and pretrite conules to mid-molar; prominent anterior pretrite conule. Specimen KNM LU 57 (reversed drawing in Fig. 10O) from **Lukeino-A** (Tassy 1986, Pl. XIII-4, Table 17). **P.** Six lophids; no talonid; moderate wear; single posterior posttrite and pretrite conules to mid-molar. Specimen L216-6 (reversed drawing in Fig. 10P) from **Kuseralee Member, Kuseralee Dora** (Table 1). **Q.** *Estimated* six lophids on complete molar; small talonid; moderately worn partial molar; *estimated* single posttrite and pretrite posterior conules to mid-molar. Specimen BC 380 from **lower Chemeron Formation. R.** *Estimated* six lophids on complete molar; small talonid; moderate wear; single posterior posttrite and pretrite conules to mid-molar; cement. PQ L-40011 (reversed drawing in Fig. 10R) from **QSM/PPM, Varswater Formation, "E" Quarry, Langebaanweg**. **S.** Six lophids; small talonid; no wear; single posterior posttrite and pretrite conules to mid-molar. No number; from **Sahabi** (Petrocchi, 1954, Pl. XIV). **T.** Estimated six, possibly seven, lophids; moderate talonid; well worn; single posterior posttrite and pretrite conules to end of molar; single anterior posttrite conule on last lophid; ectoflexus; cement. L150-1 (Fig. 13) from **upper Sagantole Formation, Wee-ee** (Table 1).

11. Right M₃ (L90-2), *Anancus kenyensis*, Bikirmali Koma, Asa Member (5 cm scale).

12. Right M₃ (L206-10), *A. kenyensis*, Kuseralee Dora, Kuseralee Member (5 cm scale).

13. Right M₃ (L150-1), *A. sp.* (Sagantole-type), Wee-ee, upper Sagantole Formation (5 cm scale).

14. Left M² (L90-1), *A. kenyensis*, Bikirmali Koma, Asa Member (5 cm scale).

15. Left M² (L224-1), *A. kenyensis*, Sagantole D'ar, Haradaso Member (5 cm scale).

16. Right M₂ (L222-1), *A. kenyensis*, Sagantole D'ar, Haradaso Member (5 cm scale).

17. Left M³ (L337-3), *A. sp.* (Sagantole-type), Bodo, upper Sagantole Formation ("Kalaloo beds") (5 cm scale).

18. Partial right M³ (L124-1), *A. sp.* (Sagantole-type), Ado Kaho Koma, upper Sagantole Formation (5 cm scale).

19. Right M² (L227-1), *A. sp.* (Sagantole-type), Beearyada, upper Beearyada beds (5 cm scale).

20. Left M² (L89-7a), *Stegotetrabelodon orbus*, Saitune Dora, lower Adu-Asa Formation (5 cm scale).

21. Length and angle of symphyses of holotype mandibles of: **a.** *Stegotetrabelodon syrticus*, **b.** *Stegotetrabelodon orbus*, **c.** *Stegodibelodon schneideri*. Adapted from: Coppens (1972); and Maglio (1973, Pl. II-4; as reconstructed from Maglio 1970a, Pl. II-5).

22. Right M² (photographed, uncollected specimen), *S. orbus*, Kuseralee Dora, Kuseralee Member (5 cm scale).

23. Edentulous mandible (L176-1), cf. *Stegodibelodon schneideri*, Adu Dora North, Adu Member (full scale length: 20 cm).

24. Left M₁ (L89-5a), *Stegodon* cf. *S. kaisensis*, Saitune Dora, lower Adu-Asa Formation (oblique view; 5 cm scale).

25. Right M₁ (L113-1), cf. *Stegodon kaisensis*, Adu Dora South, Asa Member. (Note: Width partially distorted because of oblique angle of figure; 5 cm scale).

26. Left M² (L110F-1), *Primelephas gomphotheroides*, Dofa, Asa Member (5 cm scale).

27. Right M² (L211-2), *P. gomphotheroides*, Kuseralee Dora, Kuseralee Member (5 cm scale).

28. Left M₂ (L151-1), *Loxodonta adaurora*, Wee-ee, Sagantole Formation (5 cm scale).

29. Left M₂ (?)(L123A-1a), *L. adaurora*, Wadayemero, upper Sagantole Formation (5 cm scale).

Appendix Figures

LIST OF TABLES

Appendix Table

ACKNOWLEDGMENTS

This work was made possible by our former Ethiopian and American colleagues with the RVRME who all assisted in various ways in the field documentation and recovery of fossils described in this report. In this regard, we particularly thank Sleshi Tebedge. Many contributed funds to our collective surveys and all contributed ample time and energies. To all with the RVRME we are deeply grateful. Much appreciation goes to Liz Oswald for finding the oldest elephant (L27-1), *M. subplanifrons*, thus far in the eastern Middle Awash, and for later finding the first *Anancus* (L90-1) in the Awash Valley, in late 1975, on her last day in the Afar Depression. A special word of gratitude goes to the late Douglas Cramer who was an invaluable colleague and friend during the initial explorations of much of the Middle Awash region; it was he who discovered the first "rompastompodont."

We thank those Ethiopian institutions that encouraged and supported our research in various ways, namely the Ministry of Culture, the National Museum, the Commission for Science and Technology, the Commission for Higher Education, and Addis Ababa University, which allowed us to establish the Paleobiology Research Laboratory in the Biology Department, the first such laboratory in Ethiopia.

For help in the initial identifications of fossil material we particularly thank Vincent Maglio, who also provided us with invaluable photographs of type fossils and other material; also, we are grateful to the late Michel Beden and Cary Madden. We also thank Q. B. Hendey and Meave Leakey for photographs of *Anancus* from their respective countries. One of us (JK) thanks Yves Coppens who first interested him in fossil elephants, in 1972, while with the IARE.

For valuable discussion, comments or information, we thank Vincent Maglio, Ernest Lundelius, Jr., David Froehlich, Gorden Bell, Andrew Hill, Noel Boaz, Tim Rowe, Dan Fisher, Wann Langston, Louise Roth, the late Abdel Gaziry, and particularly Kyle Davies. For technical assistance, we thank Maria Saenz, Doris Tischler, and Susan Murphy. For help in manuscript preparation at the crack of dawn and well into the night, we thank Sharon Robertson. Much appreciation for timely consideration goes to Carole Le Faivre of the American Philosophical Society.

One of us (AM) is particularly grateful to the Fulbright Scholarship Fund, the Department of Systematics and Ecology of the University of Kansas, and particularly Larry Martin and Robert Hoffman. The other (JK) is particularly grateful to the Vertebrate Paleontology Laboratory (Texas Memorial Museum), Chris Hallock, and Cindy Kehoe of the Balcones Research Center Library Service, and, for financial assistance, the Geology Foundation, all of the University of Texas at Austin. Lastly, thanks go to Judy Kalb.

INTRODUCTION

On reviewing the classification of the order Proboscidea in 1942, G. G. Simpson noted that Henry Fairfield Osborn spent much of 45 years of his life and nearly all of his last 15 years preparing his two monumental volumes on proboscideans (Simpson 1945, 244). The first volume—in press for 12 years—was published in 1936; the second volume was published seven years after Osborn's death, in 1942 (Osborn 1936, viii, 1942). The two books combined weigh nine kilograms (20 lbs.), comprise 1,675 pages and contain 1,244 illustrations. As Simpson (1945, 244) noted, "There are no more Osborns."

In the world of African vertebrate paleontology, however, there have been a select number of notable researchers whose collective works mirror both the exacting science of proboscidean paleontology and the determined efforts by many to explore the African continent. Among these individuals and some of their important works are: Pomel (1879), Andrews (1904a, 1904b), Dietrich (1915, 1941), Dart (1929), MacInnes (1942), Petrocchi (1943), Cooke (1947), Coppens (1965), Arambourg (1970), Maglio (1970a, 1973), Coppens et al. (1978), Beden (1979a, 1985), Tassy (1986), and Gaziry (1987). Among the more recent paleontologists, the efforts of Vincent Maglio stand out; his 1973 monograph, *Origin and Evolution of the Elephantidae*, represents a classic work that describes both important discoveries by Maglio and others in the 1960s in Africa and provides a major synthesis of studies of fossil elephants (Maglio 1970a, 1973). More recently, the collective works of the late Michel Beden present state of the art descriptions of the genera *Loxodonta* and *Elephas*, from such important African sites as Koobi Fora, Kenya, Laetoli, Tanzania, and the Omo Valley, Ethiopia (Beden 1983, 1987a, 1987b), as well as give important insights into the biostratigraphy and phylogeny of the Elephantinae (Beden 1985). Of the slowly growing numbers of African vertebrate paleontologists, the work of the late Abdel Gaziry (1987) of Libya represents a major contribution to the study of proboscideans from North Africa.

Much of the important early work on African proboscideans was conducted during the first half of this century accompanying widespread investigations by researchers during Africa's colonial period. Much work since then has been in tandem with large scale team efforts to investigate fossil hominid sites. One such team was the International Afar Research Expedition (IARE) working in northeastern Ethiopia in the area known as the Afar Depression. Also called the Afar Triple Junction because of the confluence of three major rifts in the region (Pilger and Rösler 1975) (Fig. 1), the area became a focal point of paleontological research by the

1

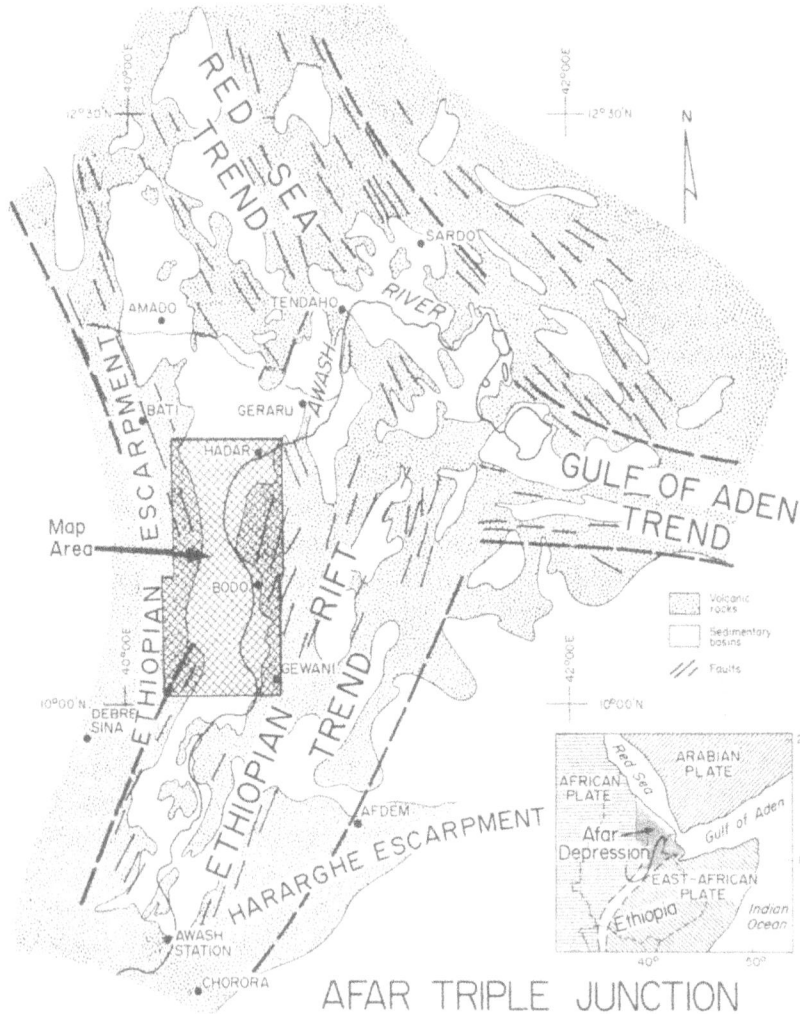

FIGURE 1. Location map of study area within Afar region, Ethiopia.

IARE in the 1970s. This work accompanied the recovery of numerous early hominids from the now famous middle Pliocene site of Hadar (Figs. 1 and 2), discovered by French geologist Maurice Taieb in 1970 (Taieb et al. 1976). These fossils were assigned to the species *Australopithecus afarensis* and include the largely complete skeleton known as "Lucy" (Johanson et al. 1982).

Unfortunately, description of the elephant fossils recovered from Hadar, and from sites to the north surveyed by the IARE (Taieb et al. 1972, 1974), remain uncompleted due to the passing in 1984 of Michel Beden, who had begun detailed studies of the IARE fossil elephants (Beden 1979b, 1981, 1985). Nevertheless, Beden's assessment revealed in detail the stratigraphic distribution at Hadar of the three major elephant genera—*Loxodonta*, *Mammuthus*, and *Elephas*—found typically in African deposits of late Pliocene age (Beden 1985; Maglio 1973) (Fig. 3).

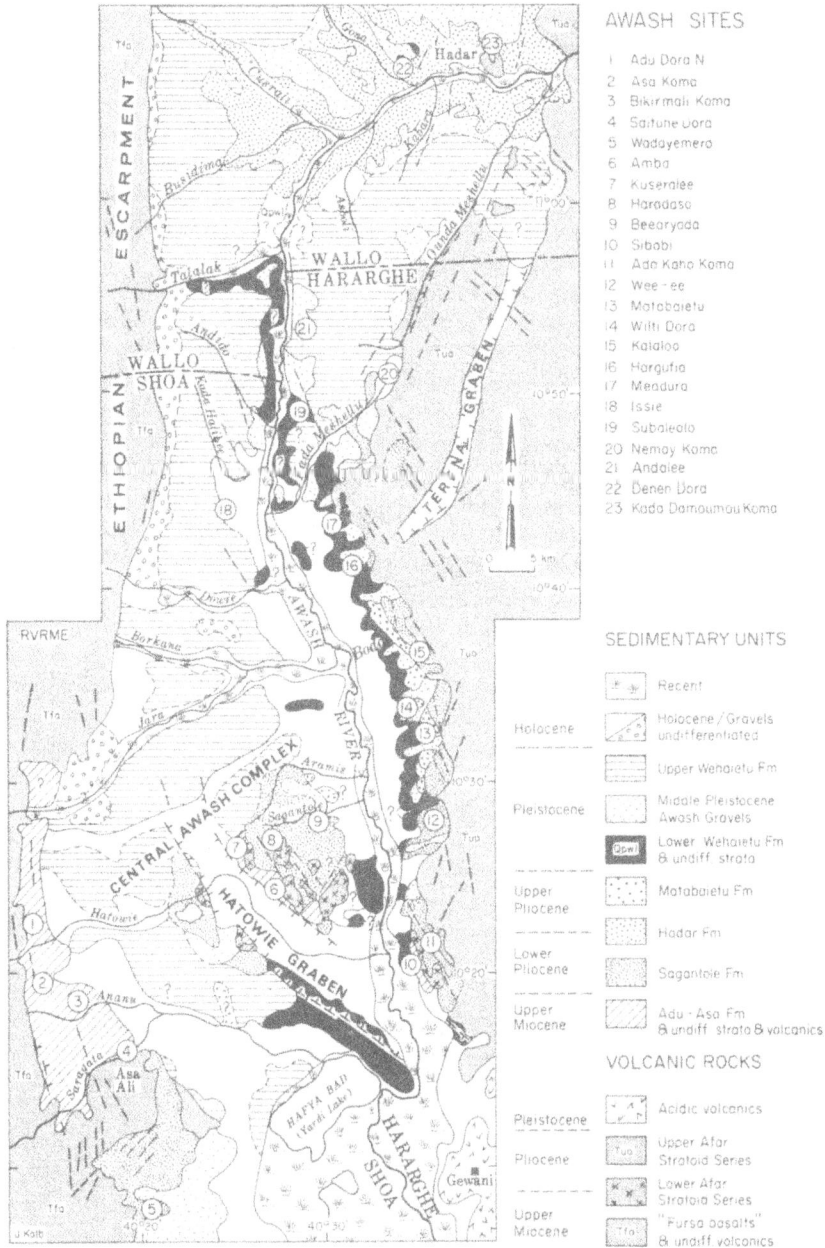

FIGURE 2. Geological map of study area.

The fossils described in this report come from the Middle Awash Valley, in Ethiopia's Hararghe and Shoa administrative regions, lying south of Hadar (Fig. 2). Much of this area was initially explored and studied from 1975–1978 by the Rift Valley Research Mission in Ethiopia (RVRME). This group was an Addis Ababa-based, American-Ethiopian organization led by one of us (JK) under the authorization of the Ethiopian Ministry of Culture. We will also refer briefly to fossil elephants

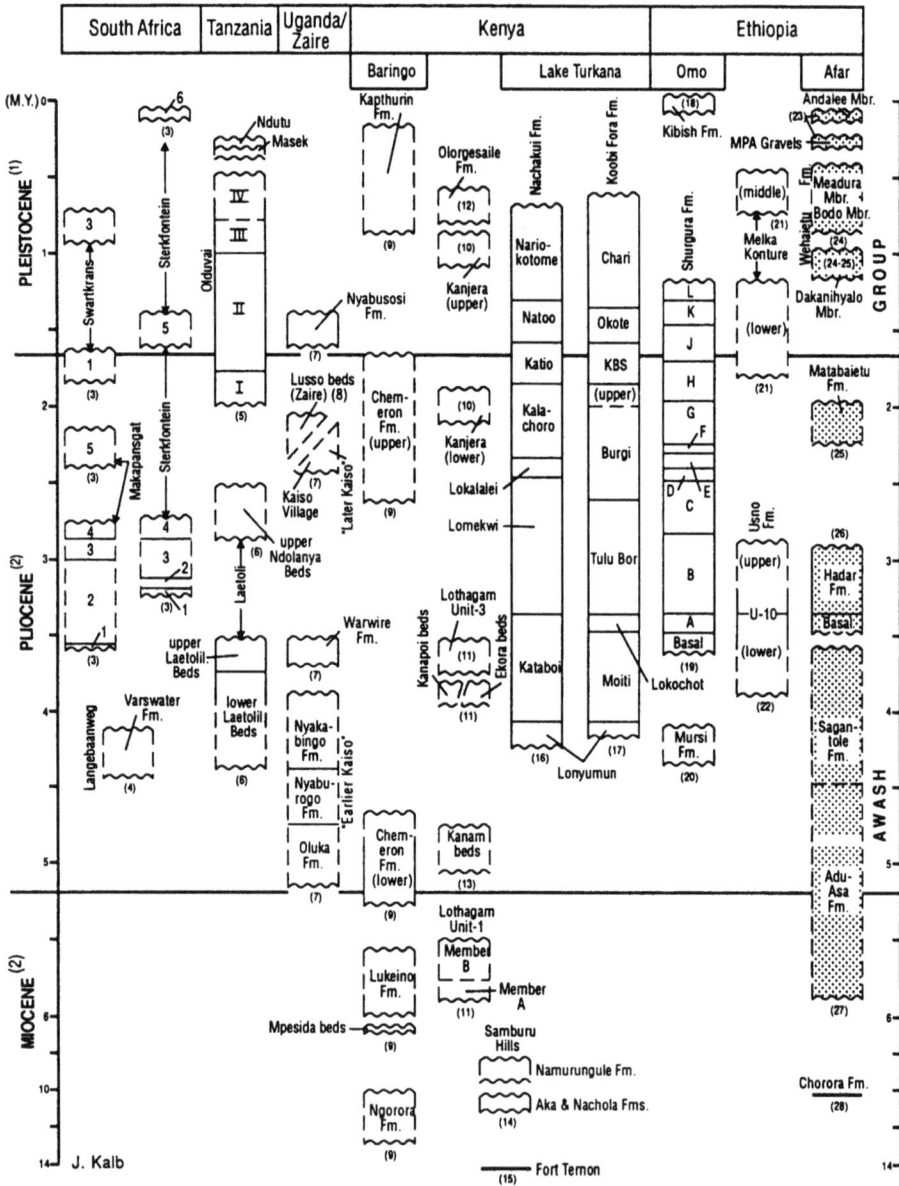

FIGURE 3. Correlation of fossiliferous deposits in Africa.

from Hadar, and to those from a scattering of sites north of Hadar surveyed by one of us (JK) from 1971–1974 while with the IARE (Kalb and Peak 1975).

Discoveries by the RVRME in 1975–1976 revealed extensive fossiliferous deposits in the Middle Awash extending far earlier than those at Hadar, comprising some 350 meters (m) of upper Miocene and lowermost Pliocene sediments, as well as over 300 m of fossil deposits younger than the Hadar beds (Kalb 1978; Kalb et al. 1982e) (Figs. 4, 5). The RVRME

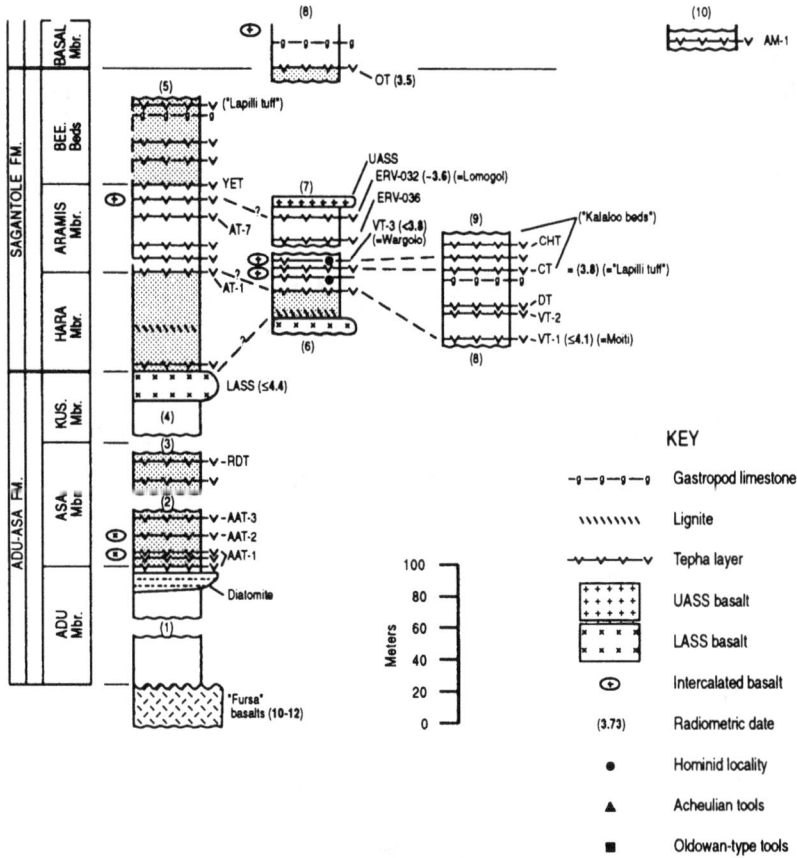

FIGURE 4. Stratigraphy of the Awash Group: the Adu-Asa and Sagantole formations.

revealed the younger beds to be often extremely rich in archeological remains, in deposits ranging from upper Pliocene to upper Pleistocene in age (Kalb et al. 1982b, 1984). Acheulian stone tool-bearing deposits may prove to be the largest single concentration of Paleolithic artifacts in Africa. The RVRME also discovered the first hominid in the Middle Awash, a largely complete cranium of archaic *Homo* recovered from the Pleistocene site of Bodo (Conroy et al. 1978; Kalb et al. 1980). Subsequent surveys in lower Pliocene deposits documented by the RVRME also produced hominid fossils reportedly similar to those at Hadar, but significantly older (Asfaw 1988; Clark et al. 1984).

Prior to the work of the RVRME, only preliminary geographical explorations had been conducted in the Middle Awash region (e.g., Nesbite 1935; Thesiger 1935). Geological studies were limited to regional mapping in the southeastern part of the area in the 1930s by two pioneering Italian geologists, Michele Gortani and Angelo Bianchi (1938, 1941a, 1941b), and photogeology by the United Nations Geothermal Project (1973) carried out in 1970–1971 by James and Demissie (1971). This work was then compiled into a regional geologic map of the Awash Valley by

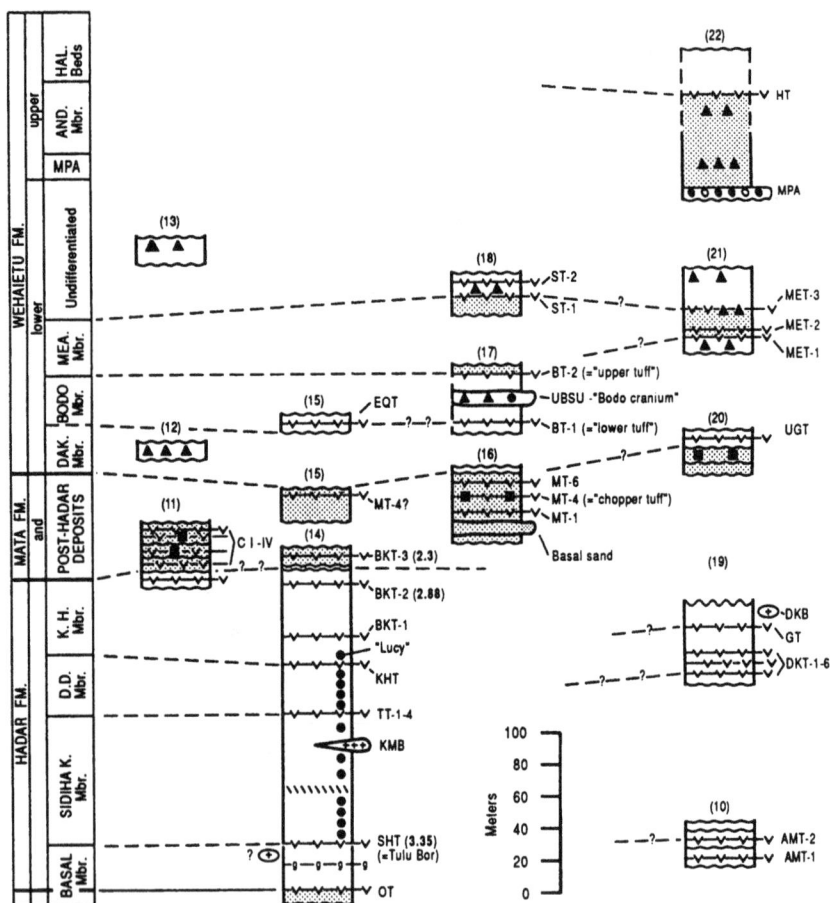

FIGURE 5. Stratigraphy of the Awash Group: the Hadar, Matabaietu and Wehaietu formations.

Taieb, who also conducted studies in the vicinity of Gewani village (Taieb et al. 1972; Taieb 1974) (Fig. 1). Subsequent to the end of fieldwork by the RVRME in 1978 for political reasons (Lewin 1983; Marshall 1987), the Middle Awash fossil and artifact sites were revisited in 1981 by a team based at the University of California at Berkeley (Clark et al. 1984). Other than fragmentary hominid fossils, however, this team collected no fossils in the Middle Awash.

Prior to the initial reports by the RVRME (Kalb 1976, 1977, 1978; Kalb et al. 1982b), no vertebrate fossils were described from the Middle Awash study area; the first fossil proboscideans were described by Mebrate (1976, 1977, 1983), Kalb et al. (1982d), and Mebrate and Kalb (1981, 1985). The work of Mebrate (1983) on the Elephantidae is the basis of his contribution to this report.

FOSSILS AND COLLECTING LOCALITIES

Some 2,500 mammalian fossils were recovered from 333 collecting localities in the Middle Awash by the RVRME. The elephantoids include the genus *Anancus*, and all recognized genera of the family Elephantidae, except *Stegolophodon*, including *Stegotetrabelodon*, *Stegodibelodon*, *Stegodon*, *Primelephas*, *Loxodonta*, *Mammuthus*, and *Elephas* (Kalb et al. 1992a). These fossils are housed in the Ethiopian National Museum in Addis Ababa.

Of the fossils recovered from the Middle Awash area, 94 specimens have been identified as elephantids, 36 as *Anancus*, and two as yet unidentified elephantoids.* These fossils come from 77 collecting localities throughout 11 named stratigraphic units of the Awash Group (Fig. 6, Table 1). At least 18 defined taxa of proboscideans have been identified from throughout the entire sequence.

Localities were documented stratigraphically with respect to measured sections, and to base maps at scales of 1:6,000 to 1:60,000 drawn from aerial photographs. Fossil localities were established with respect to discrete stratigraphic units and marker beds, nearly always represented by tephra and basalt layers, as summarized below and in Table 1 and Figures 4–6. A more detailed description of the stratigraphic distribution of the RVRME fossil localities can be found in Kalb (in press).

Individual localities seldom exceeded 100 square meters (m²) and the stratigraphic interval sampled rarely exceeded a few meters. The proboscidean fossils recovered represent only a fraction of the total number present in the localities discovered and mapped in the Middle Awash. At that, all specimens collected were surface finds. The fossils described here are confined to representative specimens in the RVRME collection; also, to those for which data are available for study since the RVRME ceased operations in Ethiopia. Further, the proboscidean fossils described are confined principally to dentition and some jaw material, since teeth are commonly well preserved and traditionally used for taxonomic purposes. Most fossils, however, including *Anancus* and elephantid skulls that could not be collected with the resources then available, were mapped, some photographed, and left *in situ* for future recovery.

---

* Molars near the base of the Middle Awash sequence are an "indeterminate gomphothere." These specimens are unworn partial molars recovered from the site of Bikirmali Koma (L97C-1, L98-1) and recorded at Asa Koma in the Asa Member (Fig. 2). They are characterized by their small size and low hypsodonty (e.g., L98-1: L = 64 mm, W = 46 mm, H = 38 mm, HI = 83 with 2½ loph(id)s), transverse arrangement of cones and conelets, V-shaped valleys, and plicated enamel cones possessing longitudinal furrows. Unfortunately, the specimens remain inaccessible at this time for further description.

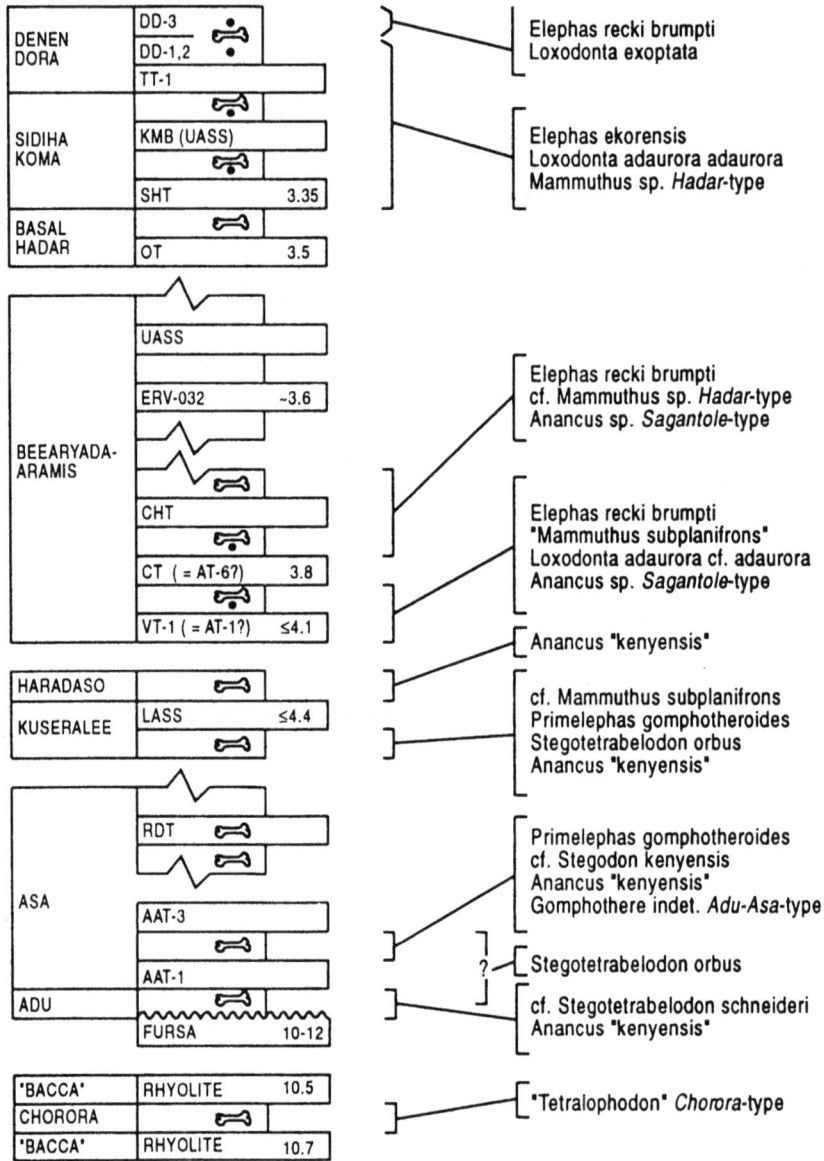

FIGURE 6. Summary stratigraphy, radiometric dates, and distribution of proboscideans in the Awash Group.

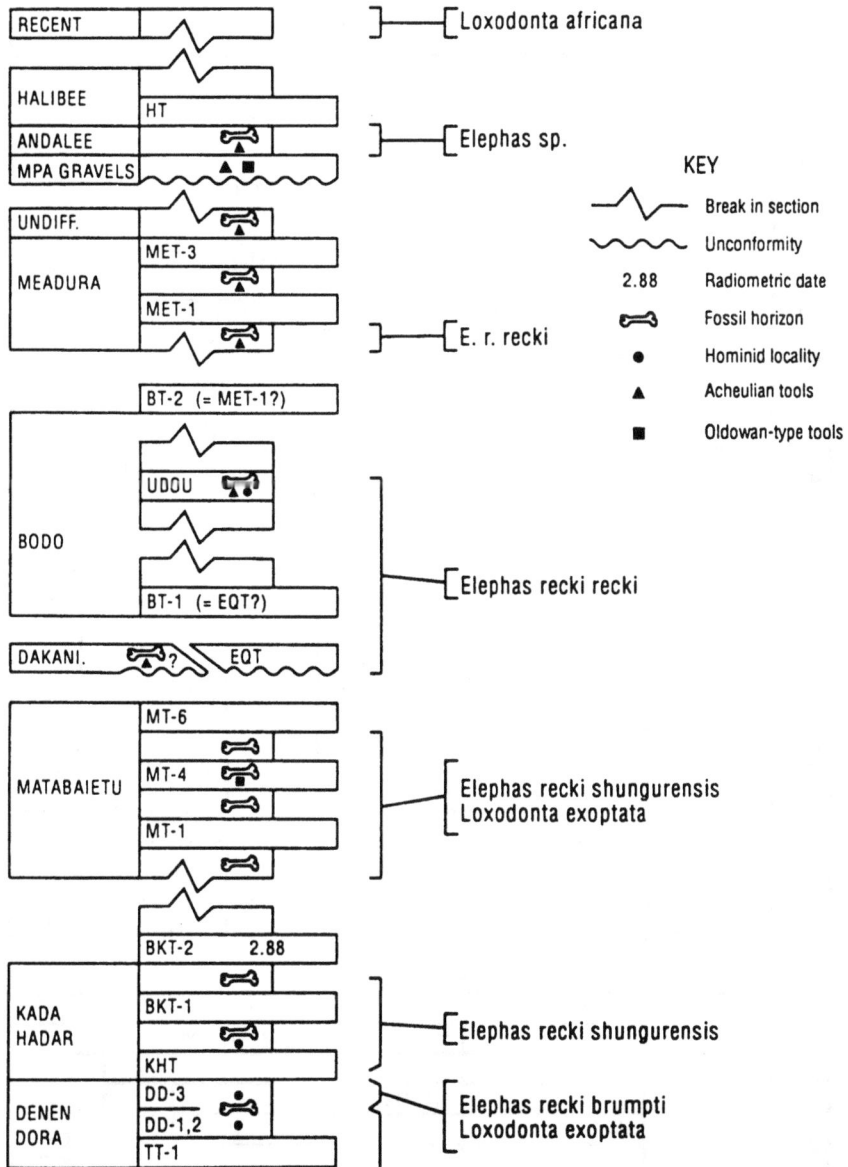

Fm.	Sub-unit	Horizon	Collecting Localities
WEHAIETU (upper)	HALIBEE	HT	
	ANADALEE		191, 192 (?)
	MPA	GRAVELS	
WEHAIETU (lower)	MEADURA	MET-1	
			80, 194, 197
	BODO	BT-2	
	BODO	UBSU	264, 283
	BODO	BT-1	
	— — —	Equus Tuff (=BT-1?)	17, 30 (at WILTIDORA)
	DAKANI.	Lower Beds	108, 109

Fm.	Sub-unit	Horizon	MATABAIETU	WILTIDORA
MATABAIETU	upper	MT-6		
			236	
	lower	MT-4 ('chopper tuff')	70	'chopper tuff' ?
			77, 239	
	lower	MT-1	4, 34, 43, 44, 59, 67, 68, 71	12, 16, 17, 23
		Basal sand	234, 243	

SAGANTOLE (Fm.)

Sub-unit	Horizon	WESTERN AWASH		WADAYEMERO	HARADASO WEST	ADO KAHO	WEE-EE	MAKA/MATABAIETU/HASANABA	'KALALOO beds'	BODO
BEEAR-YADA	upper lapilli tuff									
			227, 328					3		337
			332, 334							
	YET									CHT
ARAMIS	AT-7			121	208	124		240 - 242		246
				123		128				VT-3
	AT-6 (=CT?)					26				CT
						150 - 152		140 - 141		32, 33
						154				DT
	AT-1 (=VT-1?)					27				VT-1
HARADASO	Lignite									
			222, 224, 315, 320, 323							

Fm.	Sub-unit	Horizon	Collecting Localities		
ADU - ASA	KUSERALEE	LASS basalts			
			182, 206, 210, 211, 216, 291, 302		
	ASA	AAT-3			
			112, 113	110	SAITUNE DORA 89 ?
		AAT-2			
			90, 97, 98, 104	161	
		AAT-1			
	ADU	upper sands	170, 176		
		FURSA basalts			

TABLE 1. Fossil collecting localities in the Awash Group, Middle Awash Valley.

LOCATION AND STRATIGRAPHY

The area surveyed and geologically mapped by the RVRME comprises about 5,000 square kilometers (km²) and lies within the drainages of the Awash River north and west of Gewani village and south of Hadar (Figs. 1 and 2). The Pleistocene hominid and Acheulian tool site of Bodo lies in the central part of the region, and is part of an extensive fossil-rich Acheulian tool complex discovered by the RVRME that comprises some 35 km² of continuous archeological occurrences (Conroy et al. 1978, Fig. 1; Kalb et al. 1980, 1982b, 1982c, 1984). *(In this report, geological epoch and stage boundaries are based on Harland et al. [1990] [Fig. 3].)*

The Middle Awash region is bounded on the west by the Ethiopian escarpment, made up largely of Oligocene-Miocene volcanic rocks (Zanettin and Justin-Visentin 1974), and on the east by a plateau capped by Pliocene basalts of the Upper Afar Stratoid Series (UASS) (Varet 1978). Parts of the south-central area are capped by basalts of the Lower Afar Stratoid Series (LASS) that lie within a complexly faulted graben and horst structure referred to as the Central Awash Complex (Kalb et al. 1982c, 1982e) (Fig. 2). Most of the remaining Middle Awash region dips basinward and gently northward, reflecting progressive subsidence away from rift margins and towards the triple junction of the Red Sea, Gulf of Aden, and East African rift structures (Kalb 1978; Kalb et al. 1982c, 1982e) (Fig. 1).

Sedimentary units constitute the Mio-Pleistocene formations of the Awash Group, from bottom to top, the: Chorora, Adu-Asa, Sagantole, Hadar, Matabaietu and Wehaietu formations (Kalb et al. 1982c, 1982e) (Fig. 2-6). The entire sequence is approximately one kilometer in thickness, and ranges in age from c. 5-6 million years (m.y.) to the present, making it one of the most extensive fossiliferous sequences in Africa (Fig. 3). Vertebrate fossils representing over 175 extinct species have so far been identified throughout the group (Kalb et al. 1982d; White et al. 1984). Hominid fossils or artifacts have been documented in the upper half of the sequence, spanning a period of 4 m.y., making the Awash Group one of the most extensive records known of early hominid habitation (Kalb et al. 1982b, 1984; Harris, J. W. 1983) (Figs. 4 and 5).

The location of select collecting sites is given in Figure 2 with more detailed site information in Kalb (in press). The stratigraphic position of localities from which proboscideans were recovered is indicated in Table 1 and Figures 4-6. Individual marker beds noted in Table 1 and Figures 4-6 are discussed below.

The Chorora and Hadar formations have been described by Schönfeld

11

and Taieb respectively (*in:* Sickenberg and Schönfeld 1975; Johanson et al. 1978), while the remaining formations have been described by Kalb et al. (1982c, 1982e). Kalb (in press) has added to these descriptions with an emphasis on identifying tephra layers for purposes of further defining fossil bearing horizons, marker beds, and potentially datable tephra layers (Figs. 4–6). This work follows that of Kalb et al. (1982c, 1982e), and more recently Hall et al. (1984), Walter et al. (1985a, 1985b), and Haileab and Brown (1992), who have described and dated tuff layers in the eastern Middle Awash area between Bodo and Asaberi (Fig. 4). For purposes of this report, a brief summary of the overall Awash stratigraphy is given below, as summarized in Figures 4–6.

Chorora Formation

This unit crops out along the Hararghe escarpment in the extreme southwestern margin of the Afar region, between the villages of Awash Station and Chorora (Fig. 1). Rhyolites, within the "Bacca volcanics" bracketing this formation, have been dated at 10.5 and 10.7 m.y. (Tiercelin et al. 1979) (Fig. 6a).

Adu-Asa Formation

This formation is best exposed in the far southwestern Middle Awash Valley and is bracketed below by the "Fursa basalts" and above by the LASS basalts (Fig. 4). The former have been provisionally dated at 10–12 m.y. (Zanettin and Justin-Visentin 1974) and are unconformably overlain by sediments of the Adu Member. This member is readily distinguished by massive diatomites at the top and delimited from the Asa Member by equally massive, stratified tuffs occurring at the base of this unit. The basal tuffs, which actually comprise a compact succession of tuff layers, are referred to by Kalb (in press) as Asa Tuff (AAT)-1, while stratigraphically higher tuffs are referred to as AAT-2 and -3 (Fig. 4). The highest tuff identified in the Asa Member is the Rodent Tuff (RDT), which contains fossil rodent teeth and other small mammals within a coarse-grained, pumice tuff. In the area of the Hatowie Graben (Fig. 2), the Kuseralee Member is directly overlain by successive flows of the LASS basalts; the base of the Kuseralee Member is covered by Holocene deposits. The LASS basalts conformably overlie the Kuseralee Member and seal the Adu-Asa Formation. Reasonably, these basalts are older than 4.4 m.y., the oldest date thus far obtained from the overlying UASS basalts (Varet 1978, 23) that intercalate the middle and upper Sagantole Formation and the Hadar Formation (Figs. 4–6). Based on fauna, such as that described in this report (Fig. 6), it is clear that the Kuseralee Member is at least basal Pliocene, while the Adu and Asa Members are late Miocene in age (Kalb et al. 1982d).

Sagantole Formation

In the eastern Central Awash Complex (CAC) area the nearly non-tuffaceous Haradaso Member directly overlies the LASS basalts in faulted structures (Figs. 2 and 4). A distinctive lignite layer occurring in the middle portion of this member serves as an easily traceable marker bed, beneath which lie the fossil localities in this member documented by the RVRME (Fig. 4, Table 1). The overlying Aramis Member and the largely undifferentiated Beearyada beds in the western Awash area are distinguished by numerous tuff layers present throughout both units. Within the Aramis Member seven tuff layers (AT-1, -2 . . . . -7) have so far been identified. The base of the overlying Beearyada beds is delimited by a massive, very thick unit previously referred to as "yellow tuffs" (YET) (Kalb et al. 1982c, 104), which is derived from a waterlain basaltic ash (C. Henry, pers. com., 1990).

Near the top of the Beearyada beds in the far eastern CAC—on the *west* side of the Awash River—is a distinctive "lapilli tuff" underlain by a prominent resistant gastropod limestone, which Kalb et al. (1982c, 104–106, 1982e) have suggested may correlate with a lapilli tuff and gastropod limestone unit on the *east* side of the Awash River. The latter tuff lies at the base of the "Kalaloo beds" at Bodo (Kalb et al. 1982c, 106) and can be traced to the north and as far south as Wee-ee (Figs. 2 and 4). Hall et al. (1984) described this same lapilli tuff at Bodo in the eastern Awash area as the "Cindery Tuff" (CT) and dated it radiometrically at ≈3.9 m.y., although Haileab and Brown (1992) suggest this tuff is ≈3.8 m.y. Hall et al. (1984) also refer to underlying tuffs at Bodo and nearby areas, from top to bottom, as the Doublet Tuff (DT), Vitric Tuffs (VT)-2 and -1, and a tuff overlying the CT as VT-3 (Fig. 4). Walter et al. (1984) suggested on the basis of tephrostratigraphic correlation that the VT-1 correlates with the Moiti Tuff at Lake Turkana, which is currently dated at ≤4.10 m.y. (McDougall et al. 1985). They have also suggested that the VT-3 correlates with the Wargolo Tuff at Turkana, which Haileab and Brown (1992, Fig. 3) show to date just less than the CT (≈3.8 m.y.). These authors also imply that the VT-1 (Moiti Tuff) may be the basal tuff (AT-1) of the Aramis Member, which in turn suggests that the AT-3 and AT-4 may correlate with the DT and CT. Until tephrostratigraphic correlations can be carried out matching tephra layers on both sides of the Awash River, any identifications will remain tentative. Meanwhile, in this report fossil localities are delimited with respect to tuff layers as they are referred to and named on either side of the Awash River (Fig. 4, Table 1).

Haileab and Brown (1992) refer to a tuff near Asaberi as the ERV-032, which lies stratigraphically above the VT-3 (Fig. 4), and which they believe may compare with the Lomogol Tuff at Turkana that is ≈3.6 m.y. It may be that ERV-032, or an underlying tuff at Asaberi referred to as ERV-036, may lie stratigraphically above the uppermost tuff at Bodo, which Kalb (in press) refers to as the Channel Tuff (CHT) (Fig. 4).

Hadar Formation

Field and faunal relationships have long since indicated that the Hadar Formation lies down dip and up section from the Sagantole Formation (Kalb et al. 1982e, Fig. 5B; 1982b, Table 2; 1982c). The northward dipping Hadar beds—containing abundant hominid fossils (Johanson et al. 1982)—are bracketed below by the Oudaleita Tuff (OT), which crops out south of Hadar, and above by the Bouroukie Tuff-2 (BKT-2), which crops out in the northern Hadar area (Taieb et al. 1978; Gray 1980, 46-56) (Fig. 5). The age of the Sidi Hakoma [=Sidiha Koma] Tuff (SHT) lying near the base of the Hadar Formation—above the OT and below the Kada Damoumou Basalt (KMB)—appears secure at 3.35 m.y. This age is based on its correlation with the Tulu Bor Tuff in the Turkana Basin (Brown 1982, 1983; Haileab and Brown 1992) (Figs. 5-6). The well-known *Australopithecus afarensis* skeleton ("Lucy") lies at the base of the Kada Hadar Member just above the Kadar Hadar Tuff (KHT) and below the BKT-1; neither tuff has been reliably dated (Johanson et al. 1982, Fig. 3) (Fig. 5). Published dates for the age of the BKT-2 have varied widely (2.58-3.23 m.y.) (Walter and Aronson 1982; Hall et al. 1985; Schmitt and Nairn 1984; Walter 1989). Haileab and Brown (1992) present strong arguments for a younger age (2.88 m.y.) for the BKT-2, as originally proposed by Walter and Aronson (1982).

Two sites referred to in this report, Geraru and Amado (Fig. 1), discovered by one of us in 1973 (Kalb and Peak 1975), contain deposits that may compare in age to the upper and perhaps lower Hadar beds respectively, as preliminarily indicated by faunal evidence (Gentry 1981; Geze 1985) (Fig. 5). An assessment of the stratigraphy of Geraru tentatively suggests that the lithology of the Geraru beds may compare with the Denen Dora and Kada Hadar Members of the Hadar Formation (Kalb in press).

Matabaietu Formation

In the eastern-central Middle Awash area (Fig. 2), distinctly fluviatile, oxidized sediments of the artifact-bearing Matabaietu Formation occur in fault contact with, or are unconformable with, the often distinctly well-stratified, carbonate-rich lacustrine beds of the Sagantole Formation. At Matabaietu (Fig. 2), six tuff layers (MT-1, -2 . . . -6) are present that are highly variable and interdigitated with sands and reddish clays, a lithology also well represented at such sites as Wilti Dora, Gemeda, and Bodo (where this formation was originally referred to as the "Middle Bodo beds" by Kalb et al. 1980) (Figs. 5 and 6). The MT-4 at Matabaietu is the same as the "chopper tuff" previously referred to by Kalb et al. (1982c, 107) and contains unmistakably *in situ* Oldowan-type artifacts (Larson 1977; Kalb et al. 1982b, 1982c, 119). The MT-4 may correlate with an upper tuff at the site of Wilti Dora (Figs. 2 and 5), where Oldowan tools are found as surface occurrences, and with tuffs at the Bodo site where "Developed Oldowan" tools are reported (Harris 1983, Clark et al. 1984).

Fauna from the richly fossiliferous Matabaietu Formation indicates a post-Hadar, upper Pliocene age (Kalb et al. 1982d, Tables 2, 3), placing this unit stratigraphically proximal to very poorly fossiliferous deposits unconformably overlying the Kada Hadar Member, including those associated with the BKT-3 tuff at Hadar itself and with conglomeratic deposits at nearby Gona (Fig. 5). The latter are intercalated with four tuffs referred to by Roche and Tiercelin (1980, Fig. 2) as Cinerites (C) I–IV, which these authors suggest may overlie the BKT-2 and correlate (at least in part) with the BKT-3 at Hadar. C-I and C-IV also bracket Oldowan-tool bearing deposits reported by Corvinus (1976) and others (Corvinus and Roche 1980; Harris, J. W. 1983).

Wehaietu Formation

The lowest strata in this formation may be the Dakanihyalo Member, which crops out on the southeastern margin of the Hatowie Graben (Fig. 2). Kalb et al. (1982b, 1982c) originally estimated based on fauna that these predominantly fluviatile deposits post-date the Bodo Member. Clark et al. (1984, 416), however, suggest on the basis of artifact typology ("Lower Acheulian") and unspecified fauna that this member antedates the Bodo Member. Whatever the case, it is clear that the Dakanihyalo stone tools and fauna is post-Matabaietu in age.

The upper tuff at the site of Wilti Dora (Fig. 2) in the Matabaietu Formation (which may be the same tuff as the MT-4 at nearby Matabaietu) is unconformably overlain by the *Equus* Tuff (EQT) (Figs. 5 and 6), bearing the first occurrence of *Equus* thus far reported in the Awash Group (Kalb et al. 1982d, 241, Table 2). The EQT may correlate with the "lower tuff" at the Acheulian site of Bodo (Kalb et al. 1980, 111). This lower tuff, referred to here as Bodo Tuff-1 (BT-1) (Kalb, in press), appears to underlie (though not directly) the hominid- and stone tool-bearing "Upper Bodo Sand Unit" (UBSU) described by Kalb et al. (1980, 111) (Fig. 5). An "upper tuff" just north of Bodo (Kalb et al. 1980, 112), referred to here as the BT-2, appears to overlie the UBSU (also not directly). No radiometric dates are yet available for the BT-1 or -2, but the fauna suggests approximate correlation with fossil- and Acheulian-bearing deposits at Olorgesailie, Kenya, which appear to range in age from 0.7 to 0.9 m.y. (Bye et al. 1987; Gowlett 1987).

Ten kilometers north of Bodo at the site of Meadura (Fig. 2) the extremely prolific Acheulian stone tool deposits of the Meadura Member contain three tuff layers referred to by Kalb (in press) as the Meadura Tuffs (MET)-1, -2, and -3 (Fig. 5). The lowest tuff (MET-1) may prove to be the BT-2 although field relationships suggest this is unlikely (Kalb, in press). Likewise, the MET-3 may prove to be the lower Subalealo Tuff (ST)-1 that crops out at the site of Subalealo 10 km north of Meadura (Fig. 2).

The lower Wehaietu Formation is delimited from the upper part of the formation by the Middle Pleistocene Awash (MPA) Gravels that are ubiq-

uitous atop plateau surfaces in much of the western Awash Valley. Overlying these gravels at Andalee are the richly fossiliferous deposits of the
Andalee Member, containing a later Pleistocene "forest fauna" and "terminal" Acheulian-type ("Sangoan") stone tools (Kalb et al. 1982a), that
are separated from the overlying Halibee beds by the Halibee Tuff (HT).

SYSTEMATICS HISTORY

The cladogram in Figure 7 and associated classification in Table 2 from Kalb et al. (1992a) is the basis for the classification used in this report. The taxa listed in Table 2 for the superfamily Elephantoidea are limited to those described from the Middle Awash, as well as those referred to in discussion. Following Kalb et al. (1992a), the elephantoids are divided into the informal, paraphyletic "gomphotheres" and the monophyletic family Elephantidae (Appendix). Of the former, the genus *Anancus* is of most concern here as it is abundant in the Middle Awash. "Gomphothere" is an informal, operative term that refers to elephantoids with a distinctive bunodont dentition with a trifoliate enamel structure. In particular in this report, the term is applied only to those elephantoids referred to as "gomphotheres" in the classification of Kalb et al. (1992a) (Table 2, Fig. 7). The term does not imply a monophyletic group.

Osborn (1918) originally placed the short-jawed *Anancus* in the subfamily Brevirostrinae, which he later included within the family Bunomastodontidae and the superfamily Mastodontoidea (Osborn 1921, 1942) (Table 3). In Simpson's (1945) revision of Osborn's classification of the Proboscidea (Osborn 1936, 1942), he placed *Anancus* within the subfamily Anancinae Hay 1922, the family Gomphotheriidae Cabrera 1929, and the suborder Elephantoidea Osborn 1921. Maglio (1973) followed Simpson's revision, except he included the family Gomphotheriidae within the suborder Gomphotherioidea, as did Coppens et al. (1978) (Table 3). Based on cladistic analyses and related classification schemes, Tassy (1988, 1990), Tassy and Shoshani (1988), and Kalb et al. (1992a) include the genus *Anancus* within the paraphyletic "gomphotheres."

Other elephantoids that we describe in this report are the Elephantidae, which are well represented in the Middle Awash collection by the "stegomorphs" and the elephantines. "Stegomorph" is also an informal, operative term *only* introduced by Kalb et al. (1992a) that refers to the "stego"-prefixed paraphyletic series of taxa that lie morphologically intermediate between the "gomphotheres" and the subfamily Elephantinae (the "true elephants"). These taxa are *Stegolophodon, Stegotetrabelodon, Stegodibelodon,* and *Stegodon* (Appendix). *Stegolophodon* is the only stegomorph not known from the Middle Awash; it is arguable whether fossils belonging to this genus have thus far been recovered anywhere from Africa (Kalb et al. 1992a, 1992b).

In Volume I of *Proboscidea,* Osborn (1936, 700) placed *Stegolophodon* in the monotypic subfamily Stegolophodontinae, within the family Mastodontidae Girard 1852, and the superfamily Mastodontoidea Osborn 1921. Osborn (1936, 32–33) also put the genus *Stegodon* in its own sub-

17

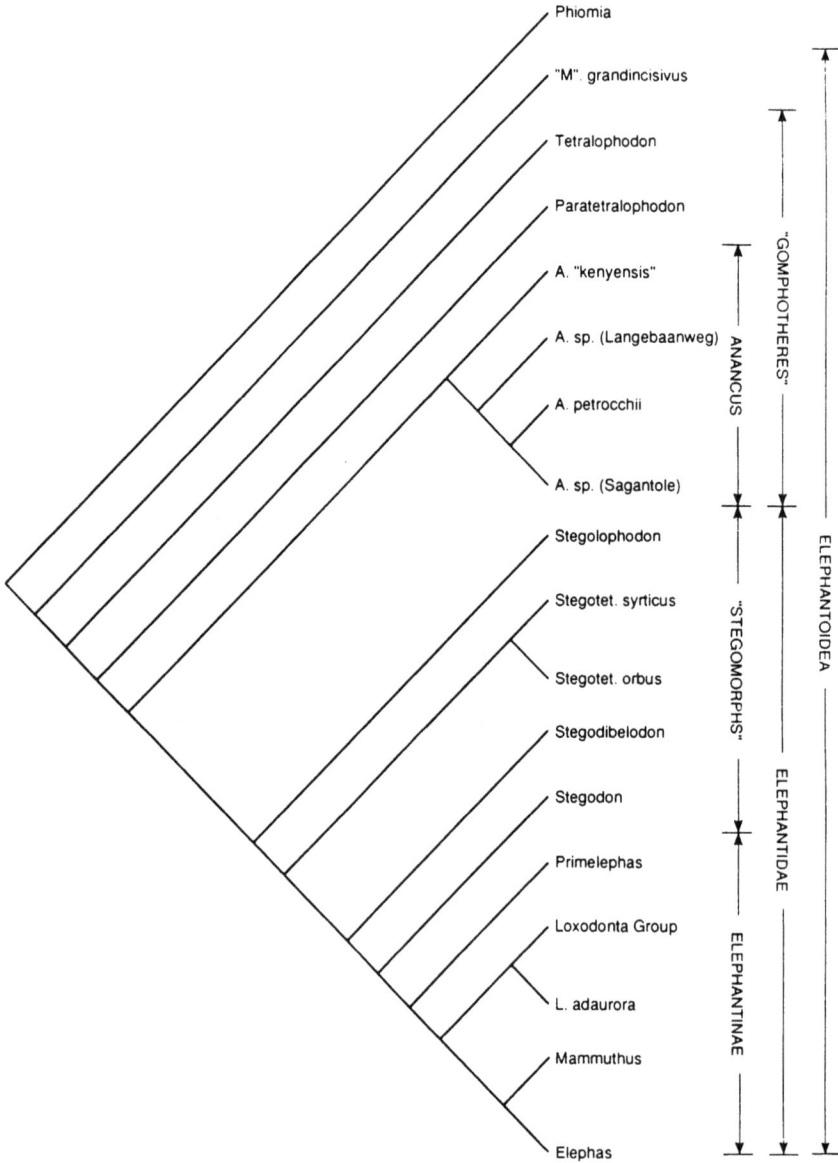

FIGURE 7. Cladogram of late Neogene Proboscidea.

family, Stegodontinae Osborn 1918, within the family Elephantidae Gray 1821 and the superfamily Elephantoidea Osborn 1921. In Volume II of *Proboscidea*, however, Osborn (1942, 1539) followed Young (1935) and Hopwood (1935) and placed *Stegodon* in its own family, Stegodontidae, which Osborn then put into the superfamily Stegodontoidea Osborn 1936 (Table 3). Simpson (1945), however, collapsed Stegodontoidea into the Elephantoidea, and incorporated Stegolophodontinae and the Stegodontinae into the Elephantidae. In doing so, he included both *Stegoloph-*

Order Proboscidea
  Suborder Elephantiformes
    "Gomphotheroids"
      Phiomia serridens
    Superfamily Elephantoidea
      "Gomphotheres"
        Plesion *"Mastodon" grandincisivus*
        Plesion *Tetralophodon longirostris*
        Plesion *Paratetralophodon hasnotensis*
        Genus *Anancus*
          Anancus "kenyensis"
          Anancus sp. (Langebaanweg-type)
          Pentalophodont *Anancus* Group
            Anancus petrocchii
            Anancus sp. (Sagantole-type)
    Family Elephantidae
      "Stegomorphs"
        Plesion *Stegolophodon*
        Genus *Stegotetrabelodon*
          Stegotetrabelodon syrticus
          Stegotetrabelodon orbus
        Plesion *Stegodibelodon schneideri*
        Plesion *Stegodon*
    Subfamily Elephantinae
      Plesion *Primelephas gomphotheroides*
      Genus *Loxodonta*
        Loxodonta Group
          "cf. *Loxodonta*" (Lukeino-A type)
          L. exoptata
          L. atlantica
          L. africana
        Loxodonta adaurora
      Unnamed Group
        Genus *Mammuthus*
        Genus *Elephas*

TABLE 2. **Classification of late Neogene Proboscidea used in this volume.**

odon and *Stegodon* in the subfamily Stegodontinae (Simpson 1945, 133, 245–249). Maglio (1973) and later Coppens et al. (1978), however, placed the two genera in the family Stegodontidae, which they included in the suborder Mammutoidea (Table 3). The monophyletic status of *Stegolophodon* and *Stegodon* has most recently been maintained by Tassy (1988, 1990) and Tassy and Shoshani (1988). Taruno (1985), however, treats *Stegolophodon* as a member of the family Gomphotheriidae and retains *Stegodon* within the family Stegodontidae, along with *Eostegodon* Yabe 1950, a Jap-

OSBORN, 1942

Order Proboscidea
　Superfamily Mastodontoidea
　　Family Bunomastodontidae
　　　Subfamily Ambebelodontinae
　　　　Genus *Phiomia*
　　　Subfamily Tetralophodontinae
　　　　Genus *Tetralophodon*
　　　Subfamily Brevirostrinae
　　　　Genus *Anancus*
　　Family Mastodontidae
　　　Subfamily Stegolophodontinae
　　　　Genus *Stegolophodon*
　Superfamily Stegodontoidea
　　Family Stegodontidae
　　　Subfamily Stegodontinae
　　　　Genus *Stegodon*
　Superfamily Elephantoidea
　　Family Elephantidae
　　　Subfamily Mammontinae
　　　Subfamily Loxodontinae
　　　Subfamily Elephantinae

COPPENS ET AL., 1978

Order Proboscidea
　Suborder Gomphotherioidea
　　Family Gomphotheriidae
　　　Subfamily Gomphotheriinae
　　　　Genus *Phiomia*
　　　　Genus *Tetralophodon*
　　　Subfamily Anancinae
　　　　Genus *Anancus*
　　Family Elephantidae
　　　Subfamily Stegotetrabelodontinae
　　　　Genus *Stegotetrabelodon*
　　　　Genus *Stegodibelodon*
　　　Subfamily Elephantinae
　　　　Genus *Primelephas*
　　　　Genus *Loxodonta*
　　　　Genus *Mammuthus*
　　　　Genus *Elephas*
　Suborder Mammutoidea
　　Family Stegodontidae
　　　Genus *Stegolophodon*
　　　Genus *Stegodon*

SIMPSON, 1945

Order Proboscidea
　Suborder Elephantoidea
　　Family Gomphotheriidae
　　　Subfamily Gomphotheriinae
　　　　Genus *Phiomia*
　　　　Genus *Tetralophodon*
　　　Subfamily Anancinae
　　　　Genus *Anancus*
　　Family Elephantidae
　　　Subfamily Stegodontinae
　　　　Genus *Stegolophodon*
　　　　Genus *Stegodon*
　　　Subfamily Elephantinae
　　　　Genus *Loxodonta*
　　　　Genus *Mammuthus*
　　　　Genus *Elephas*

TASSY, 1988

Order Proboscidea
　Suborder Elephantiformes
　　Plesion *Phiomia*
　　Superfamily Elephantoidea
　　　Plesion Gomphotheres
　　　Plesion Stegodontidae
　　　Family Elephantidae
　　　　Plesion Stegotetrabelodon
　　　　Subfamily Elephantinae
　　　　　Plesion *Stegodibelodon*
　　　　　Plesion *Primelephas*
　　　　　Genus *Loxodonta*
　　　　　Plesion *Mammuthus*
　　　　　Genus *Elephas*

TABLE 3. **Classification of late Neogene Proboscidea.**

anese form he regards as more conservative than *Stegodon*. Kalb et al. (1992a) also believe *Stegolophodon* and *Stegodon* to be paraphyletic, even distantly related, with *Stegolophodon* being the sister taxon of all other elephantids and *Stegodon* being the sister taxon of the elephantines (Appendix) (Fig. 7).

Petrocchi (1943, 1954) described the four-tusked *Stegotetrabelodon* as a monotypic genus of the subfamily Stegotetrabelodontinae (Tobien 1978a, 194); Coppens (1972) added the two-tusked *Stegodibelodon* to this same subfamily. Both Coppens (1972) and Maglio (1973) regarded Stegotetra-belodontinae as a subfamily of the Elephantidae, although Maglio (1973, 17, footnote 5) was not convinced that *Stegodibelodon* differed generically from *Stegotetrabelodon*. Coppens et al. (1978), however, included *Stegodibelodon* within the Stegotetrabelodontinae (Table 3). The monophyly of *Stegotetrabelodon* and *Stegodibelodon*, however, has been challenged by Tassy and colleagues in various papers (see Tassy 1990), although they do not resolve the cladistic relationships of these genera with other elephantids and the early elephant, *Primelephas*. Kalb et al. (1992a), however, propose that *Stegotetrabelodon* and *Stegodibelodon* are part of a paraphyletic series bracketed by the more plesiomorphic *Steglolophodon* and the more derived *Stegodon* (Table 2, Fig. 7).

Subsequent to Simpson's (1945) revision of Osborn's (1942, 1540) final classification of the Elephantidae, Maglio (1973) and Coppens et al. (1978) restricted the elephants to the subfamily Elephantinae, inclusive of the ancestral *Primelephas* (Maglio 1970a), *Loxodonta*, *Elephas*, and *Mammuthus* (Table 3). Tassy (1988, 1990) and Tassy and Shoshani (1988) show *Stegodibelodon* forming a dichotomy with *Primelephas*. These authors also believe *Elephas* and *Mammuthus* to be sister taxa, as inferred by Maglio (1973, Fig. 7) and Coppens et al. (1978, Fig. 17.2), and argue that the *Elephas/Mammuthus* clade is the sister group of the loxodonts. Kalb et al. (1992a) show *Primelephas* to be the sister taxon of all other elephantines (Fig. 7). However, they suggest that when more complete fossil material is available for *Primelephas* that the genus may prove to be the sister taxon of the *Mammuthus/Elephas* clade. Also, they suggest that the loxodonts may share a common ancestor with, and hence may be the sister group of, a *Primelephas/Mammuthus/Elephas* clade. Kalb et al. (1992a) also suggest that *Loxodonta adaurora* is the sister taxon of all other loxodonts, which they refer to as the "*Loxodonta* Group." They suggest that *L. adaurora* may not be the ancestor of all other loxodonts as suggested by Maglio (1973); rather they propose that this species shares a common ancestor with the *Loxodonta* Group. Otherwise, they show that the *Loxodonta* Group is a clade comprised of "cf. *Loxodonta*" from Member A of the Lukeino Formation (Lukeino-A), Kenya (Tassy 1986, Pl. XIV, Fig. 6), *L. exoptata*, *L. atlantica*, and the extant *L. africana*, all of which share a unique enamel loop envelope structure (Kalb et al. 1992a, see Appendix I) (Table 2).

TERMINOLOGY AND IDENTIFICATION

The terminology used in this report to distinguish features of *Anancus* dentition is from Tassy (1986, Fig. 2, Pl. 8) and Tobien (1973, 116–119); that used to distinguish features of elephantid dentition is from Maglio (1973, 8–13), as illustrated in Figures 8 and 9, respectively. Most of the criteria used to identify the taxa in this report, based around a cladistic framework, are discussed in detail in Kalb et al. (1992a). Of the proboscideans identified in the Awash Group, the dentitions of the two major groups present, *Anancus* and the elephants, typify the extremes of molar development of the elephantoids. The cheek teeth of the genus *Anancus* are characteristically bundont or bunolophodont, while those of elephants are fully lophodont or plate-like, as characterized in Figures 8 and 9. The number of loph(id)s on molars of *Anancus* are characters used to help distinguish species within this group as are the number of plates in elephant molars. *Anancus*, whose intermediate molars (dP4, M1, M2) have a maximum of four loph(id)s, are referred to as being *tetralophodont*, as with early forms of *Anancus*, while those with a maximum of five loph(id)s are referred to as being *pentalophodont*, as with derived forms of *Anancus* (Tobien 1973, 129). These terms are also sometimes used by authors to describe the number of plates of early elephantid molars (e.g., Tobien 1978, 177).

When describing *Anancus* molars:

Pretrite refers to the side of the molar that is *most* worn, while *posttrite* refers to the side that is *least* worn (Tobien 1973, 119, footnote; Vacek 1877, 6, footnote) (Fig. 8).

When identifying the position of *Anancus* molars in the jaw, the pretrite half-lophids of *lower* molars are on the buccal side, while the pretrite half-lophs of *upper* molars are on the lingual side.

On lower molars, the inner posttrite half-lophids occupy a more *anterior* position with respect to outer pretrite half-lophids.

On upper molars, the inner pretrite half-lophs occupy a more anterior position with respect to outer posttrite half-lophs.

Hence, inner half-loph(id)s on both upper and lower molars of gomphotheres always occupy a more anterior position (Tobien, 1973, 130).

The enamel loops of worn half-plates of elephantids display a similar though more subtle configuration as half-loph(id)s of *Anancus* with respect to the anterior position of inner half-plates.

As Maglio (1973, 89) explains, for molars of "gomphotheres" the first, more deeply, and broadly worn *pre*-trite ("*first* worn") cones serve as a grinding mortar for the secondarily worn *post*-trite cones. The terms pre-

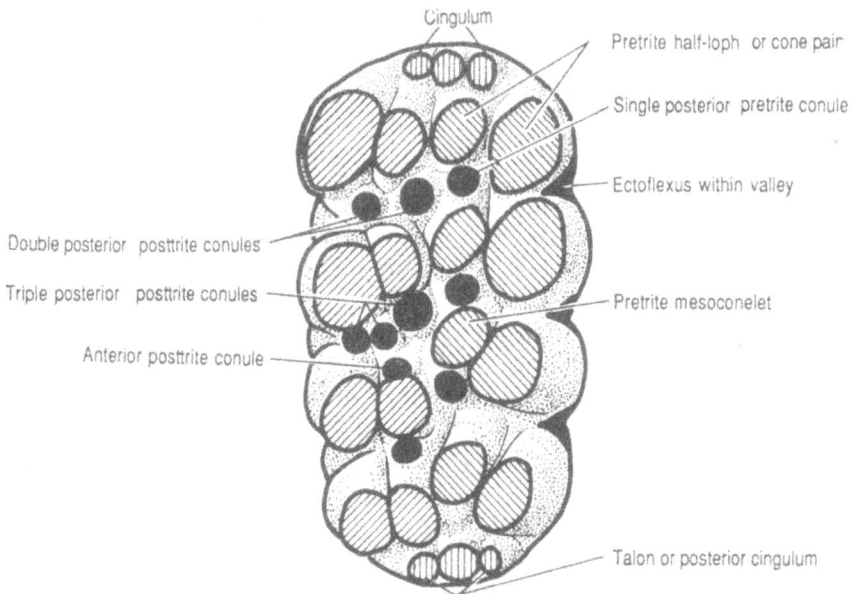

FIGURE 8. Nomenclature for *Anancus* molars.

trite and posttrite are also sometimes applied by authors to elephantid molars, although the mastication process for elephantid dentition (as opposed to gomphotheres) consists of a fore-and-aft grinding-shearing function (Maglio 1972, 1973, 89–91).

In this paper, we use the following nomenclature with reference to the direction of curvature of the opposing faces of enamel loops of worn lophids or plates, as seen when viewing the occlusal surface of molars. As described below, such curvature on *lower* molars is a single feature that distinguishes molars of *Anancus* and early elephantids from elephantines.

When the face of an enamel loop is *anteriorly* curved, it is referred to as *convex* (e.g., Figs. 20 and 30); when the face is *posteriorly* curved, it is *concave* (e.g., Figs. 9 and 38).

If opposing faces of the enamel loop are both convex, as in worn upper and lower molars of *Anancus* and *Stegotetrabelodon*, and upper molars of *Elephas*, for example, the enamel loop is referred to as *convex-convex*.

In molars of both *Anancus* and elephantids, the terms convex and concave are applied to the total configuration created by the joining or confluence of worn half-loph(id)s or half-plates.

If opposing faces of the enamel loop are both concave, the enamel loop is *concave-concave*, as readily seen in worn lower molars of *Primelephas*, *Elephas*, *Mammuthus*, and *Loxodonta adaurora*.

Finally, if the anterior face of an enamel loop is convex and the posterior face of the same enamel loop is concave, as seen in *well worn* lower molars of all loxodonts except *L. adaurora*, that is, the *Loxodonta* Group, then the enamel loop is *convex-concave* (Kalb et al. 1992a, Appendix I).

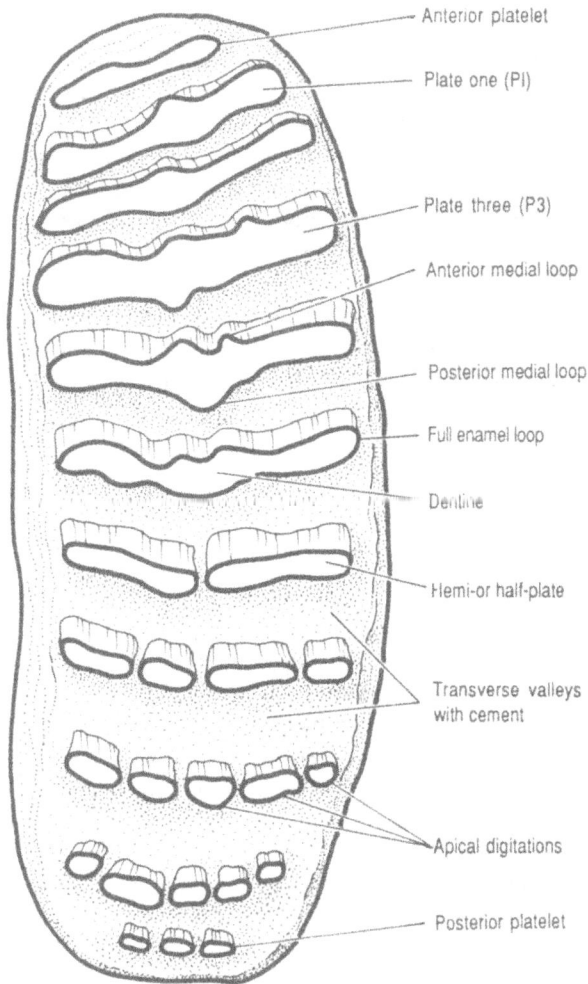

FIGURE 9. Nomenclature for elephantid molars.

Thus, plate curvature helps to identify the type of molar, as well as its taxon. Direction of curvature may sometimes be subtle depending on molar wear; in such cases, curvature may be best noticeable at the lateral margins of plates.

Curvature of enamel loops of molars is commonly enhanced or altered by incorporation of one or more intravalley *conules* into the enamel loop of loph(id)s of *Anancus,* or incorporation of *columns* (as relic conules) into the enamel loops of plates of elephantids. The number and position of these accessories significantly determines the shape of the enamel loop and is useful for the identification of taxa (Kalb et al., 1992a). As viewed on the occlusal surface of molars, the pattern of plate curvature and the arrangement of columns also facilitates the identification of individual molars (e.g., left M_1, right M^3, etc.). Conules/columns vary both in position and number with the length of the molar. For *Anancus* and elephantids, posterior conules/columns are always dominant on the pretrite side of the molar, that is, the buccal side of the lower molars and the lingual side of upper molars. In *Anancus*, posterior posttrite conules may extend no further than the mid-region of the molar, or conules may extend along the full length of the molar, either in single or double rows, and in derived species, in triple rows at the anterior end of the molar. Distinctions in loph(id) and conule development in *Anancus* molars are illustrated in Figure 8. In elephantids, columns also vary with the length of the molar, being more dominant or isolated in more ancestral forms. Columns are commonly attached to the plate at the mid-height region of the molar, being absent at the very base of the plate and at the very top (e.g., Beden 1979a, 78–84). Hence, columns may be altogether absent on very worn molars and recessed on unworn molars.

The following summarizes the criteria used for the identification of molars, with respect to their placement in the jaw and for taxonomic purposes.

For *Anancus*, inner half-loph(id)s always occupy a more anterior position on upper and lower molars.

This same condition is present in elephantids, although not as accentuated, by the anteriormost position (based on longitudinal offset) of the lingual half-plate with respect to the buccal half-plate, on both upper and lower molars.

The anterior and posterior faces of enamel loops of *Anancus* and "stego-morphs" are always *convex-convex* (except *Stegodon*, whose enamel faces may be straight or sub-parallel). This condition refers to *worn*, adjoining half-loph(id)s or half-plates.

Enamel loops of lower molars of elephants are always *concave-concave*, or *convex-concave* in the case of well worn molars of all loxodonts except *L. adaurora*. For upper molars, the posterior face of the enamel loop is always *convex*.

Convexity and concavity may be best expressed at the lateral margins of the enamel loops.

For *Anancus*, posterior conules are always dominant on the buccal (pretrite) side of lower molars, and the lingual (also pretrite) side of upper molars.

Posterior columns, as relic conules, are positioned similarly on the lower and upper molars of elephantids.

Maglio (1973, 11–12) provides detailed description of methods of metric analysis of *Stegotetrabelodon* and elephant molars, which is further useful for distinguishing taxa. We have adopted Maglio's procedure in this report, *both with regard to techniques used for measuring molars and in the metric analysis of taxa* (see Maglio 1973, 8–13). Molar features that show modifications with time particularly lend themselves to metric comparison, such as: the number of plates; relative number of plates per 100 millimeters (mm) of molar length, or the lamellar frequency; enamel thickness; crown height; maximum width; and the relative crown height, or hypsodonty index (H/W × 100).

SYSTEMATIC DESCRIPTION

ABBREVIATIONS

BC	Baringo, Chemeron Formation
IARE	International Afar Research Expedition
KE	Kanam East
KNM	Kenyan National Museum
KP	Kanapoi beds
LU	Lukeino Formation
LU-A	Lukeino Formation, Member A
LT	Lothagam Formation
PQ	Pelletal Phosphorite and Quartzose Members (undifferentiated), "E" Quarry, Langebaanweg
RVRME	Rift Valley Research Mission in Ethiopia
SAM	South African Museum

Concerning metric analysis:

ET	Enamel thickness
H	height
HI	hypsodonty index
P	plate
W	width

SYSTEMATIC DESCRIPTION

The following descriptions were greatly aided by original photographs, many unpublished, of African elephantids kindly provided by Vincent Maglio. Photographs, many unpublished, of *Anancus* molars from sites in Kenya and from Langebaanweg, South Africa, were kindly provided us by Meave Leakey of the National Museums of Kenya and by Q. B. Hendey of the South African Museum respectively.*

Superfamily ELEPHANTOIDEA Osborn 1921
Genus *ANANCUS* Aymard 1855

This short-jawed genus is characterized by its straight upper tusks and the "anancoidy" of cone pairs of its molars. The latter feature is particularly apparent on worn molars and is distinguished by alternating and interlocking pretrite and posttrite half-loph(id)s (Tobien 1973, 130). *Anancus* is reported from deposits of late Miocene to early Pliocene age over much of Africa, ranging from Morocco to Egypt (Arambourg 1970; Petrocchi 1943, 1954), Chad and Ethiopia (Coppens 1965; Mebrate and Kalb 1985; Beden 1976), and East Africa and South Africa (Tassy 1986; Hendey 1978; Coppens et al. 1978).

Anancus occurs throughout the Adu-Asa and Sagantole formations, over an estimated time range of probably not less than 1½ m.y., from the upper Miocene ($\approx$ 5.5 m.y.) in the Adu Member to the top of the Sagantole Formation (<3.8 m.y.) (Fig. 6a). Previously, we have described four time-successive stages or forms of *Anancus* based on the number of cone pairs, and the complexity and size of the molars (Kalb et al. 1982d). Subsequently, we assigned three of these stages, "Stages A–C," to *A. kenyensis*, and "Stage D" to a very progressive and previously undescribed *Anancus* (Mebrate and Kalb 1985). Below, we emend and expand these descriptions. We do so using current information on the nature and occurrence of *Anancus* elsewhere in Africa, based largely on the recent comprehensive study of the genus *Anancus* by Tassy (1986), the work of Kalb et al. (1992a), and on photographs of *Anancus* molars made available to us from sites in Kenya and South Africa.

---

* Individual specimens from these sources are referred to parenthetically by specimen number, or published reference when available.

29

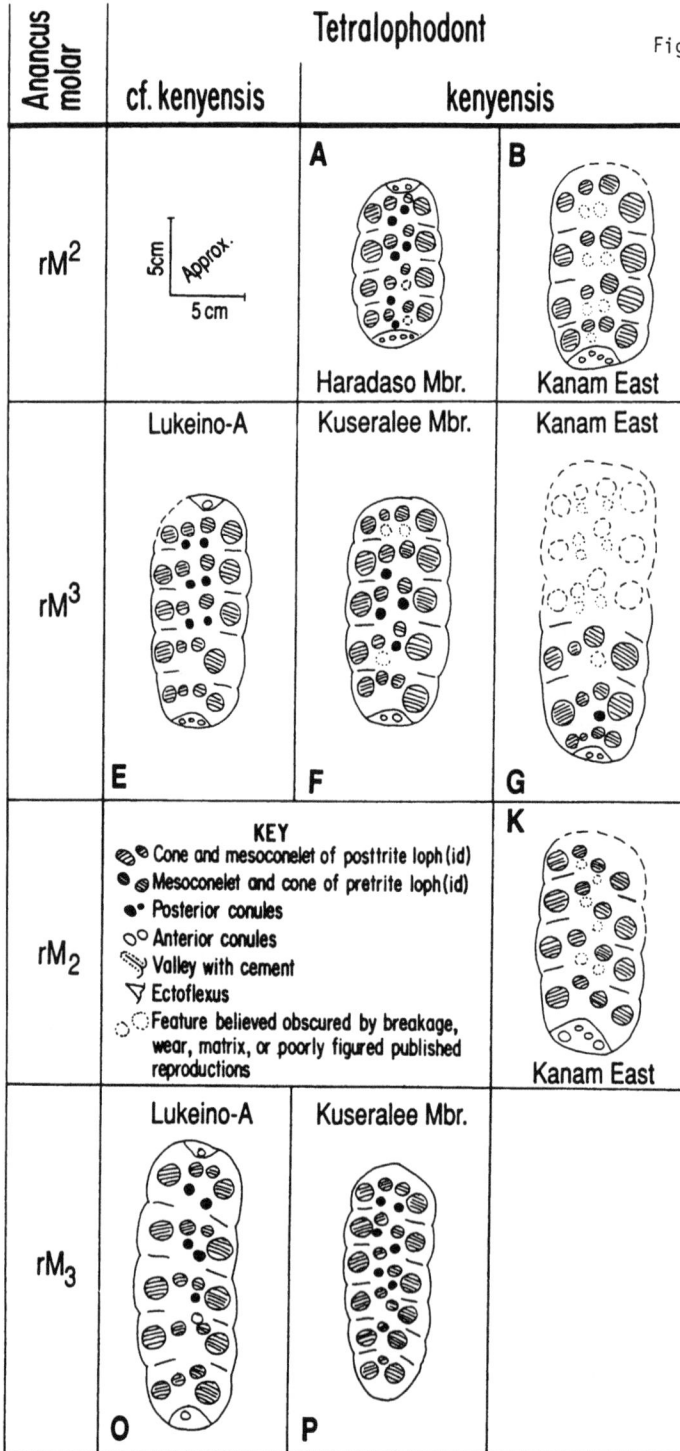

FIGURE 10.   Schematic figures of tetralophodont and pentalophodont *Anancus* molars.

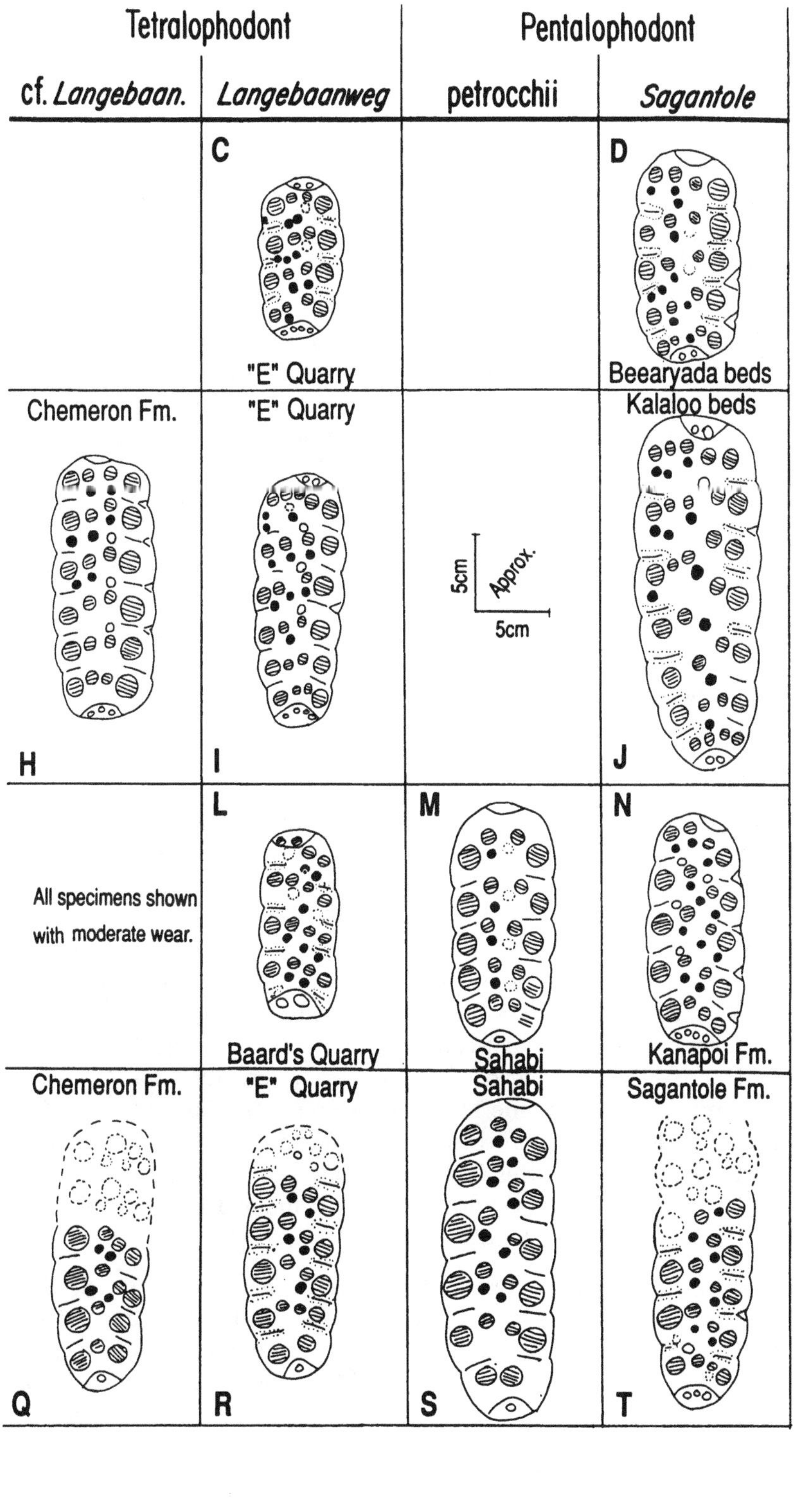
Tetralophodont
Pentalophodont
cf. Langebaan.
Langebaanweg
petrocchii
Sagantole
C
"E" Quarry
D
Beearyada beds
Chemeron Fm.
"E" Quarry
Kalaloo beds
5cm
Approx.
5cm
H
I
J
L
M
N
All specimens shown with moderate wear.
Baard's Quarry
Sahabi
Kanapoi Fm.
Chemeron Fm.
"E" Quarry
Sahabi
Sagantole Fm.
Q
R
S
T

Fig. 10b

ANANCUS KENYENSIS (MacInnes) 1942
(Figs. 10–12, 14–16)

Specimens/Localities: RVRME Locality (L) 170-1, M3(?) fragment, Adu Dora North, Adu Member; L90-1, left M^2, L90-2, partial right M_3, Bikirmali Koma (Hill), Asa Member; L216-6*; left M_3, Kuseralee Dora (Wadi), L206-10, right M_3, L206-11a,b*, right and left M^3, L206-12*, right and left M^3, Gulubahsin Dora, Kuseralee Member; L222-1, right M^2, L224-1, left M^2, L323-1, partial left M^3 Sagantole D'ar (Stream), Haradaso Member (Figs. 2–6, Table 1).

Description: L90-2 from the Asa Member is a partial right M_3 consisting of 4½ unworn posterior lophids, but no talonid (Fig. 11). The extreme wear on the anterior lophs of a left M^2 (L90-1) described below (Fig. 14) of this same individual, and the absence of anterior wear on L90-2, suggest that L90-2 had a worn sixth lophid. No posterior posttrite conules are apparent on the preserved lophids of L90-2, although posterior pretrite conules extend to the mid-molar. L90-2 is generally similar to M_3 from the Kuseralee Member, a complete left M_3 (L216-6) with six lophids (Fig. 10P) and an incomplete right M_3 (L206-10) with five lophids (Fig. 12). In terms of size, the length and maximum width (L ≈ 160 mm, W ≈ 58 mm) of L216-6 is similar to that of L90-2 (L = 113+ mm, W = 60 mm), although both molars are somewhat smaller than L206-10 (L = 135+ mm, W = 63 mm) from the Kuseralee Member. The estimated lengths of L90-2 and L206-10 on the complete molars is probably close to 155 mm and 170 mm respectively (Figs. 11, 12).

Paired M^3 from the Kuseralee Member, L206-11a,b, have five lophs, and possess single, posterior central posttrite and pretrite conules extending to the mid-region of the molars (Fig. 10F). Unfortunately, M3 known thus far from the lower Sagantole Formation are fragmentary. However, a partial left M^3 (L323-1) from the Haradaso Member with four unworn posterior lophs appears to be like L206-11 from Kuseralee.

L90-1, L222-1 and L224-1 are all tetralophodont M^2 with modest talons and single posterior posttrite and pretrite conules extending the length or nearly the length of the molars (Figs. 10A, 14–16). In size, L224-1 and L222-1 from the Haradaso Member are larger (L = 106–111 mm, W = 61–70 mm) than L90-1 (L = 96 mm, W = 68 mm) from the Asa Member, although this distinction may not be meaningful.

L170-1 from the Adu Member is a worn molar fragment (M3?) consisting of a partial cone pair.

Discussion: L90-2 characterizes the simplest M_3 in the Awash series, featured by the least development of conules and the absence of a talonid. Tassy (1986, 88–89) recognized that confinement of posterior posttrite conules to the anterior end of the M_3 is a distinguishing feature of *early A. kenyensis*, or of what Tassy refers to as the "*kenyensis*-morph" (see

---

* Denotes uncollected, but photographed specimens.

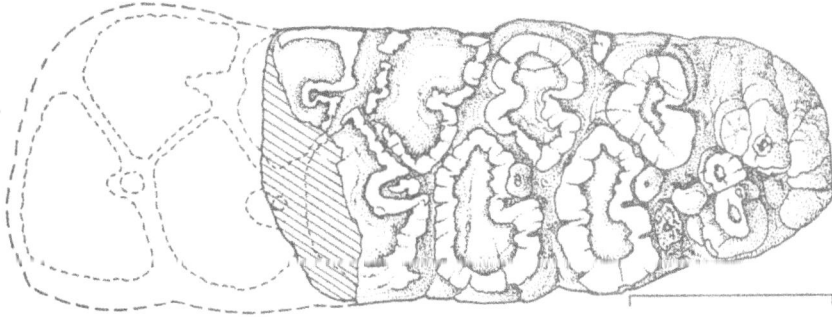

FIGURE 13. Right M$_3$ (L150-1).

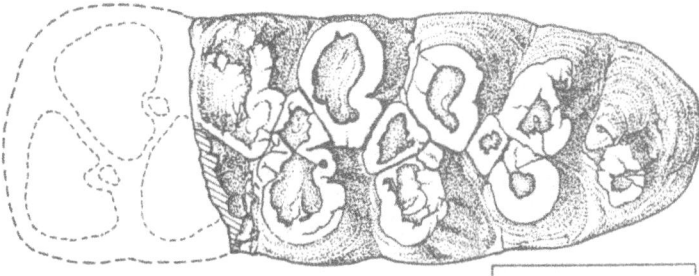

FIGURE 12. Right M$_3$ (L206-10).

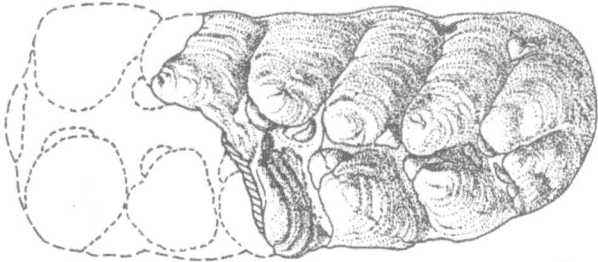

FIGURE 11. Right M$_3$ (L90-2).

[SCALE = 5 CM]

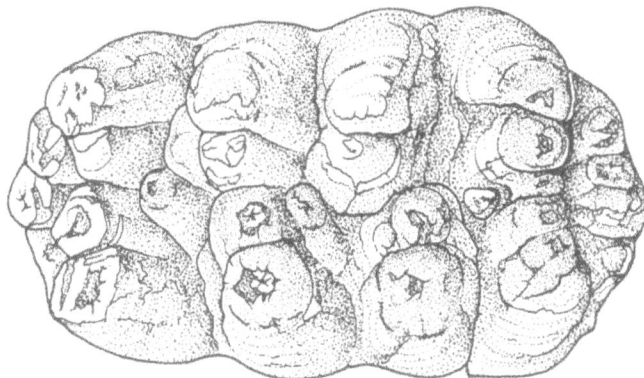

FIGURE 16.   Right M₂ (L222-1).

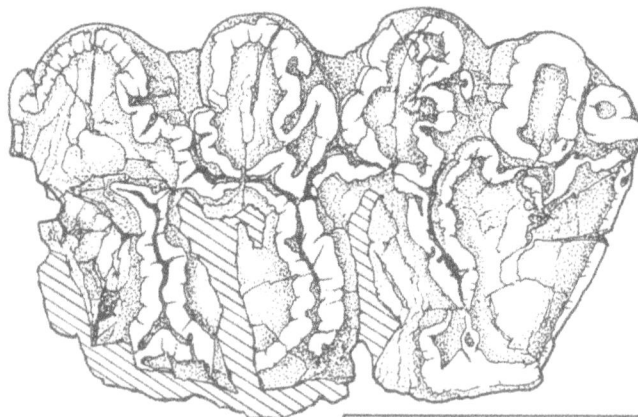

FIGURE 15.   Left M² (L224-1).

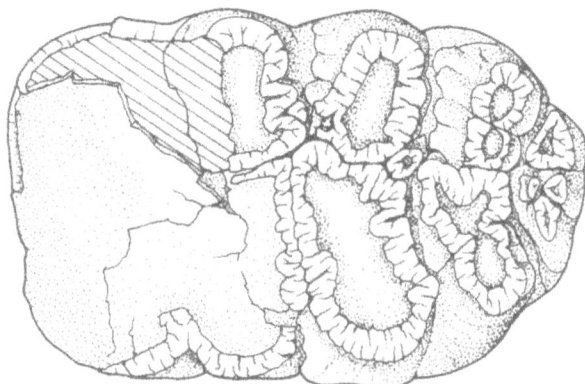

FIGURE 14.   Left M² (L90-1).

[SCALE = 5 CM]

Fig. 10O–P). With respect to posterior conule development, L90-2, L206-10 and L216-6 compare with M_3 from Lukeino-A (Fig. 10O) and the lower Chemeron Formation, Kenya (Fig. 10Q), although the Lukeino M_3 have a *minimum* of five lophids (Tassy 1986, Table 17) while the latter probably had six lophids on the complete molar. L216-6, L90-2 and L206-10 are significantly smaller than M_3 from Lukeino-A (e.g., KNM-LU-57) (L = 197 mm, W ≈ 78 mm) (Tassy 1986, Pl. XII-2, XIII-4) (Fig. 10O–P). As Tassy (1986, Figs. 36–37) has demonstrated, however, such variation suggests that size is not readily a reliable factor for distinguishing forms of late Miocene-early Pliocene *Anancus*.

The M^3 from the Kuseralee and Haradaso members are like figured M^3 from Lukeino-A and -B (Tassy 1986, Pl. XIII-1 and -2). The enamel of the Lukeino molars, however, as seen in the worn molars from Lukeino-A (Fig. 10E) appears consistently thicker, which may signify environmental and dietary differences. Both the Kuseralee and Haradaso M^3 are broadly similar to a partial unworn right M^3 (KE-24) from Kanam East (Fig. 10G), which MacInnes (1942, 82, Pl. VII-6) designated as the paratype of *A. kenyensis*. The latter, however, possesses a posterior pretrite conule near the end of the molar and is appreciably larger in size, as the holotype M^2 (KE-20) of *A. kenyensis* (Fig. 10B) is larger than M^2 described below from the Asa and Haradaso members (Figs. 10A, 14–16). It is also reasonable that the paratype M^3 from Kanam East had six lophs on the complete molar (Fig. 10G), unlike the Kuseralee M^3 documented so far which have five lophs (Fig. 10F). With respect to cone pair and conule development, the Kanam East M^3 may compare more with an M^3 (KNM BC-33) with six lophs and multiple anterior conules from the lower Chemeron Formation at Baringo (Fig. 10H). Only recovery of complete M^3 from Kanam East, however, will reveal the full morphology of the *A. kenyensis* paratype.

With regard to M^2, the holotype M^2 (KE 20) of *A. kenyensis* (Fig. 10B) is significantly larger (L = 139 mm, W = 81 mm) than the M^2 (L = 96–111 mm, W = 61–70 mm) from the Asa or Haradaso members and has a more developed talon, like an M_2 (KE-21) from Kanam East (MacInnes 1942, Pl. VII-4-5, Table, 84) (Fig. 10K). Maglio (pers. com., 1975) has suggested that the stage of development of L90-1, and L90-2 (the M_3 from the Asa Member), are similar in development to *Anancus* molars from Bed 1 of the Lothagam Group (Lothagam-1), which Coppens et al. (1978) regard as more primitive than "typical" *A. kenyensis*. Unfortunately, photographs of M2, or M3, of *Anancus* from Lothagam have not been available to the authors, that is, if such molars have been recovered from the site. Otherwise, the holotype M^2 and the M_2 of *A. kenyensis* described by MacInnes are so worn that conule development can only be estimated (Fig. 10B,K).

With regard to the molar fragment (M3?), L170-1, from the Adu Member, it is the earliest *Anancus* recovered thus far from the Awash Group, and is likely to be the same form as that from the Asa Member.

Skull and postcranial fossils have been found in the same sites as the above specimens, particularly in the Asa and Kuseralee members. One especially complete skull (in 1976) from Kuseralee that was photographed displays straight upper tusks and a fully brevirostrine lower jaw, features that typify the genus.

ANANCUS sp. (Sagantole-type)
(Figs. 10, 13, 17–19)

Specimens/Localities: L150-1, right M_3, eastern Wee-ee Dora, L140-1, partial right M_3, Matabaietu Dora South, Aramis Member(?); L337-3*, left M^3, eastern Bodo, Aramis Member(?) (upper "Kalaloo beds"); L124-1, partial right M^3, Ado Kaho Koma, Aramis Member(?); and L227-1, right M^2, Beearyada, upper Beearyada beds, Sagantole Formation (Figs. 2–6, Table 1) (see footnote on p. 32).

Description: L150-1 from Wee-ee is a large (L = 157+ mm, W = 72+ mm), worn, partial right M_3 with three posterior posttrite half-lophids, five pretrite half-lophids, and a strong divided talonid (Fig. 13). The M_3 had at least six lophids when complete, with a minimum length of ≈215 mm. Judging from the number of lophs (seven) on an M^3 from Bodo (L337-3) (Fig. 17), which we believe belongs to the same species, L150-1 may well have had seven lophids when complete, since lower molars of *Anancus* usually have the same or fewer lophs than the lophids of upper molars. Single posterior posttrite and pretrite conules are present the length of L150-1, although conules are largely incorporated into the worn lophids (Fig. 10T). An additional abaxial posttrite conule is present posterior to the fifth lophid. The fifth lophid also has a prominent anterior posttrite conule, and an ectoflexus is preserved between the fourth and fifth pretrite lophids. The enamel is thick, strongly folded, with cement present between lophids.

L140-1 from the site of Matabaietu is a large anterior molar fragment of a right M_3, with a cingulum, a single cone pair, and a single central posttrite conule. The lophids are elongate, compressed, segmented and transverse. The width of L140-1 (W = 73 mm) is similar to that of L150-1 (W = 72+ mm).

L337-3 from the uppermost Sagantole beds at eastern Bodo (Table 1) is a very large (L ≈ 230 mm, W ≈ 92 mm), complete left M^3 that is moderately worn (Figs. 10J, 17). The molar was not collected but was photographed and (in 1978) was attached to a largely complete cranium. The M^3 consists of seven lophs and a small talon. Partially worn lophs in the mid-region of the molar are widely separated, elongated, and narrow; also they are transversely oriented in a shallow, chevron-like convex-convex fashion. Lophs are segmented into a series of binary and tertiary conelets characterized by wavy enamel when worn. Pretrite and posttrite mesoconelets form almost continuous transverse structures on the occlusal surface and central posterior posttrite conules are prominent the length of the molar. Additional abaxial posttrite conules are present posterior to the first three half-lophs; a central pretrite conule is present ante-

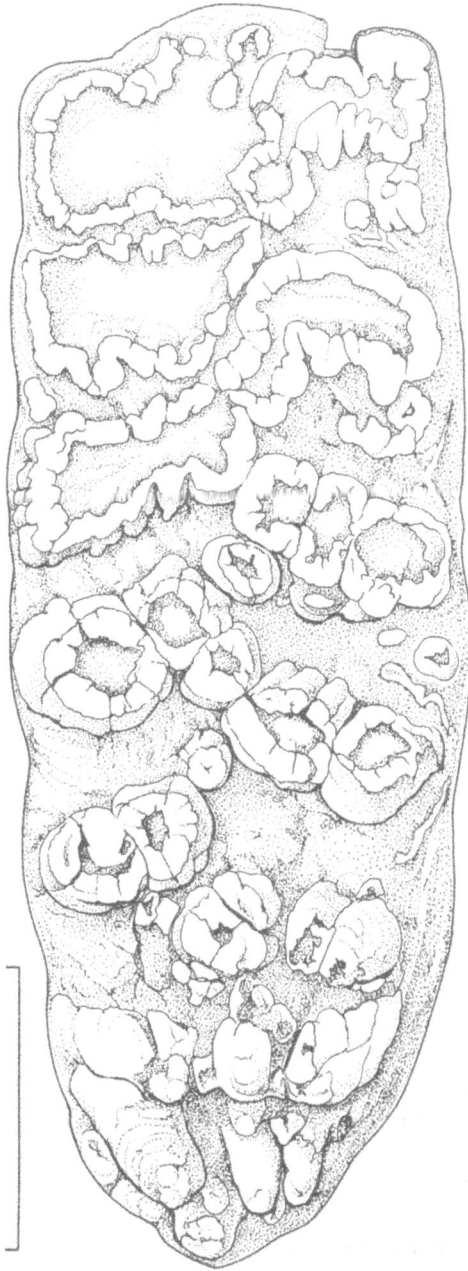

FIGURE 17. Left M³ (L337-3),
A. sp. (Sagantole-type), Bodo,
upper Sagantole Formation
("Kalaloo beds").

[SCALE = 5 CM]

rior to the second pretrite half-loph. Lophs are well separated by cement filling valleys. An endoflexus is present between the second and third pretrite lophs. Recovery and removal of matrix, which partially fills the valleys of the molar, may reveal additional accessory features, as may additional complete M³ specimens of this form.

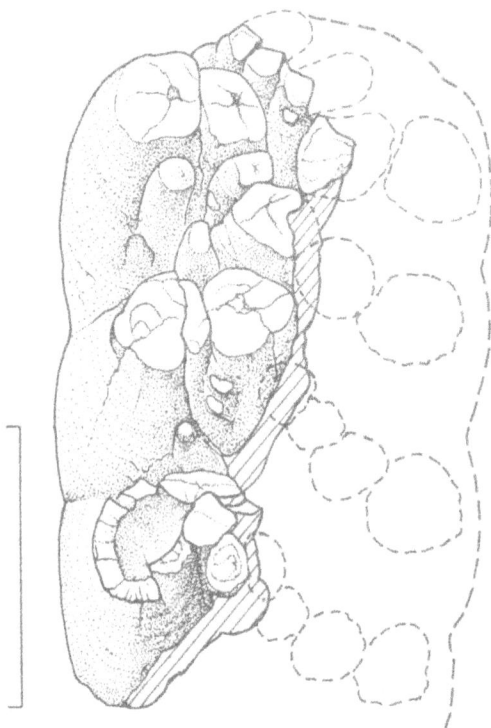

FIGURE 18. Partial right M³ (L124-1), *A. sp.* (Sagantole-type), Ado Kaho Koma, upper Sagantole Formation.

[SCALE = 5 CM]

L124-1 is an anterior molar fragment of a right M³ consisting of a partial cingulum and three slightly worn, nearly complete anterior posttrite cone pairs (Fig. 18). L124-1 is very large (L = 120 mm, W = 51 mm) and similar to L337-3 both in morphology and size. The specimen has a partial anterior pretrite mesoconelet but is otherwise broken along the midline of the molar. Central posttrite conules are preserved posterior to the first and third posttrite half-lophs; additional abaxial conelets are present posterior to the first and second posttrite half-lophs.

L227-1 is a very large (L = 142 mm, W = 75 mm), complete right M² with five moderately worn lophs and a small, divided talon (Figs. 10D, 19). Central posttrite and pretrite conules are present the length of the molar. The overall configuration of the opposing faces of the half-lophs is convex-convex, particularly on the third loph. A second central posttrite conule posterior to the first loph was probably present on the unworn molar, but is now incorporated into an extended posttrite loop. An abaxial posterior posttrite conule is strongly developed at the buccal margin of the first loph; two additional abaxial conules are present posterior to the third loph. Posterior pretrite conules the length of the molar were probably present on the unworn molar. Endoflexus ridges are present between the posterior pretrite lophs. The enamel is coarsely folded, of moderate thickness, and lophs are separated by cement.

Discussion: On the basis of the criteria described in Kalb et al. (1992a) for derived characters of progressive *Anancus*, L150-1, L337-3, L124-1, and

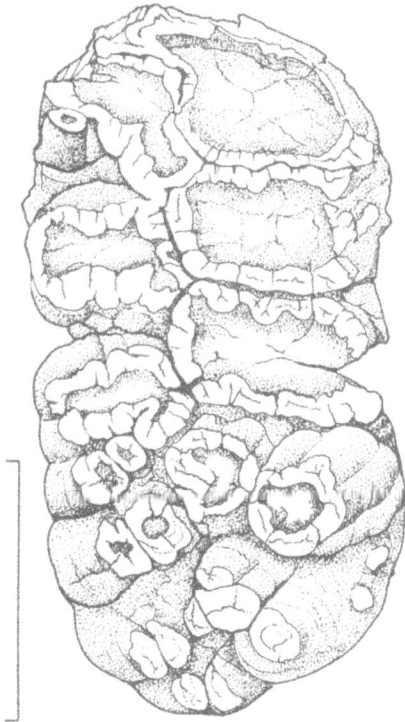

FIGURE 19. Right M² (L227-1),
A. sp. (Sagantole-type),
upper Beearyada, Beearyada beds.
[SCALE = 5 CM]

L227-1 from the upper Sagantole Formation are all clearly more progressive than *A. kenyensis* from Kanam East and the Middle Awash (Appendix). The M³ (L337-3) and the M² (L227-1) have additional lophs, seven and five respectively; it may be that L150-1 (the M₃) had seven lophids on the complete molar. A continuous increase in loph(id) (and plate) number in increasingly more progressive species of gomphotheres and other elephantoids has been well documented (e.g., Tobien 1973, 129; Maglio 1973, 642). Also, unlike *A. kenyensis*, L150-1 has posterior posttrite conules that extend the length of the molar, a derived feature, while L337-3 and L124-1 have multiple posttrite conules posterior to the anterior lophs, also a derived feature. In this respect, L227-1, the pentalophodont M², has three conules posterior to the first and third posttrite half-lophs.

It is possible that a left M₂ from Kanapoi (KNM KP-384) may belong to this same form (Fig. 10N). This specimen is also pentalophodont, with a talonid, and has central posterior posttrite conules nearly the length of the molar; also, supplementary posterior and anterior posttrite and pretrite conules extend to the mid-region of the molar. It is possible that on the unworn molar, L227-1, like the Kanapoi M₂, displayed posterior as well as anterior pretrite conules. Finally, L337-3, L227-1 and L150-1 all have cement in the valleys, which is absent in East African *A. kenyensis* (and in the Kanapoi M₂). Generally, increased cement development in elephantoids is a derived condition, although there is considerable variation in this regard (Tobien 1973, 130).

In terms of conule development, the Sagantole *Anancus* compares with an undescribed *Anancus* from the Pelletal Phosphorite and Quartzose Sand members (undifferentiated) (PQ) of the Varswater Formation, "E" Quarry, Langebaanweg (Hendey 1970b) (Fig. 3). M^2 of the latter (PQ-L41692 and PQ-L40012), however, are tetralophodont (Fig. 10C), as is a more progressive M_2 (L1179) from stratigraphically younger beds from nearby Baard's Quarry (Hendey 1978, Fig. 1) (Fig. 10L). Also, the South African M^3 have six instead of seven lophs (Fig. 10I), like L337-3; it is likely that an incomplete M_3 from "E" Quarry had six lophids when whole. Like the Sagantole molars, those from Langebaanweg also have cement in the valleys, although some specimens do not, which probably relates to environmental and stratigraphic differences between the units of the Varswater Formation.

Reasonably, the Sagantole-type pentalophodont is a new species of a very progressive pentalophodont *Anancus*, and the Langebaanweg-type *Anancus* is a new species of a very progressive tetralophodont *Anancus* (Appendix) (Fig. 7). Since a fully representative collection of the Middle Awash form will likely be possible with further fieldwork, which can include recovery of the Bodo *Anancus* skull and others, formal description of this new pentalophodont should await this prospect. The Sagantole M_3 (L150-1) and the pentalophodont M_2 from Kanapoi compare generally with *A. petrocchii* from the Sahabi Formation, Libya. However, the Kanapoi molar has distinctly greater conule development compared to that described for the Sahabi M_2 (Petrocchi 1954; Tassy 1986). Unfortunately, the Sahabi M_2 and M_3—the only molars described from this site— are poorly figured (Petrocchi 1954, Pl. 8–14) and these specimens, or quality photographs of these fossils, have not been accessible for study, even to Libyan paleontologists (A. W. Gaziry, pers. com., 1989). Nevertheless, based on the evidence available, it is likely that complete M_3 eventually recovered from the Sagantole beds will show greater lophid, and perhaps greater conule, development compared to the Sahabi M_3.

Undescribed *Anancus* from the lowermost Laetolil Beds with "greater number of lophs" reportedly compare with the Kanapoi pentalophodont *Anancus* (Hay 1987, 25; Harris, J. M. 1987, 525), and therefore, most likely with the Sagantole pentalophodont as well. We note that the lowermost Laetolil Beds bearing *Anancus* are estimated to be 4.3 m.y. (Hay 1987, 28), an age near enough to the Sagantole beds (>3.6–4.1 m.y.) bearing the Middle Awash pentalophodont *Anancus* (Figs. 3 and 6a).

Family ELEPHANTIDAE Gray 1821
Genus *STEGOTETRABELODON* Petrocchi 1941
STEGOTETRABELODON ORBUS Maglio 1970a
(Figs. 20, 22)

Specimens/Locality: L89-6b, left jaw and molar fragment, L89-7a, left M^2, L89-8, partial left M_3, Saitune Dora, lower Adu-Asa Formation (Asa Member?) (Figs. 2–6, Table 1).

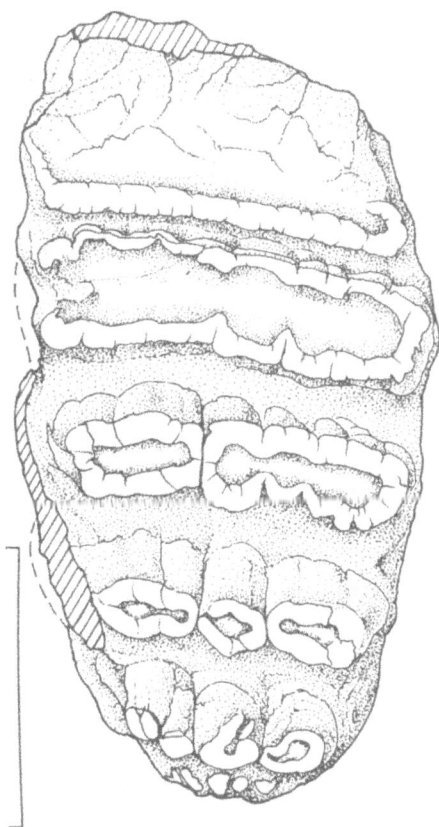

FIGURE 20. Left M² (L89-7a),
Stegotetrabelodon orbus, Saitune Dora,
lower Adu-Asa Formation.

[SCALE = 5 CM]

Description: L89-7a is a complete left M² with five plates, a very small posterior platelet, and a largely complete root (Fig. 20). The tooth is chipped along the lingual margin. The enamel loops have a shallow convex-convex shape with no preserved intra-valley columns, on a molar heavily worn anteriorly. The anterior half of the P1 is worn beneath the enamel. The P2 consists of a full broad loop; the remaining plates are segmented by median clefts. The clefts form two constrictions on the P2, two hemi-plates on the P3, and broad, thick pillars on the P4 and P5. Shallow longitudinal grooves superficially divide the plates. The tooth is 145 mm long, and low crowned (45 mm) with low hypsodonty (54). The estimated width (85 mm) is greatest on the P2 and P3. Plate spacing is wide (LF = 4), and valleys are broadly V-shaped and partially filled with cement.

L89-8 is an incompletely erupted partial left M₃ in a jaw fragment. It consists of the posterior 3½ plates of a molar that probably had seven plates when complete. The anterior plate, probably the P3, is broken and consists of a half loop with a prominent pillar fused to the buccal (pre-trite) posterior side. The worn second plate forms a complete full loop with two constrictions as remnants of median clefts; a second buccal column is fused to the posterior face of the loop. Both plates are subparallel, but with a very shallow convex-convex shape that is most apparent at the lateral margins. The third plate, with no posterior columns apparent, consists of four apical digitations partially divided by superficial grooves; four undivided digitations make up the heel of the molar. The maximum width is 68 mm, the plates are widely spaced (LF = 4) with thick enamel (4–6 mm), and they are separated by shallow valleys partially filled with cement.

L89-6b is a left lower jaw fragment with the last plate of a fully erupted M_3. Its anterior location relative to the base of the vertical ramus indicates that L89-6b is a mature adult, more so than L89-8.

Discussion: L89-7a is comparable to M^2 of *Stegotetrabelodon* from Sahabi, Libya (specimen 1P7A) (Gaziry 1987, Fig. 15) and Lothagam, Kenya (KNM LT 354) (Maglio and Ricca 1977, Pl. 1, Fig. 6). This genus and the species, *S. syrticus*, were first described from Sahabi by Petrocchi (1941), who placed it in the subfamily Stegotetrabelodontinae based on the intermediate nature of *Stegotetrabelodon* with respect to "gomphotheres" and elephants (Petrocchi 1954, 41; Tobien 1978a, 194). Petrocchi made this distinction based on the very prominent downturned, straight lower tusks (*tetrabelodont*) of *S. syrticus* (Fig. 21) and on the elephantine-like construction of its molars. Maglio (1970a, 1973) later described a second species of *Stegotetrabelodon*, *S. orbus*, from Unit-1 at Lothagam (Fig. 3) and supported Aguirre's (1968, 1969) view that the genus is an early member of the family Elephantidae, a position followed by Coppens et al. (1978) and Tassy (1986). Maglio distinguished *S. orbus* partly on its smaller size ($\approx$ 12 percent) and the reduced mandibular incisors of the holotype; however, the size distinction of the incisors is less than is apparent since the Lothagam mandible belongs to a subadult individual with worn M_2 and unworn M_3, while the holotype mandible of *S. syrticus* is a full adult with M_3 only (Maglio 1970a, 5, 1973, Pl. II-3; Petrocchi 1954, Pl. III-1) (Fig. 21). An undescribed anterior lower jaw fragment (L89-7b) recovered from Saitune Dora (that has been unavailable for this study) possesses the posteriormost end of a large mandibular symphysis that appears to have been strongly downturned, similar to those of *S. syrticus* and *S. orbus*.

Like the M^2 of *Stegotetrabelodon* from Libya and Kenya, L89-7a from Saitune Dora has median clefts, broad thick enamel loops, and five plates. L89-7a and the Lothagam M^2 (KNM LT-354) are smaller (L = 145 mm, W = 83 mm, and L $\approx$ 161 mm, W $\approx$ 93, respectively) than the M^2 (1P7A) from Sahabi (L = 172 mm, W = 90 mm), but are more comparable in size to an uncollected but photographed M^2 (L219-4) (L $\approx$ 150 mm, W $\approx$ 70 mm) from the site of Kuseralee in the Kuseralee Member (Fig. 22).

L89-7a and the Sahabi M^2 (1P7A) lack isolated intra-valley columns, but these molars are well worn, particularly the M^2. The Lothagam M^2 (KNM LT 354) possesses prominent single lingual (pretrite) columns posterior to plates (P) 2–4; the Kuseralee M^2 possesses a fused column posterior to the P4. As mentioned above, columns are present in the anterior

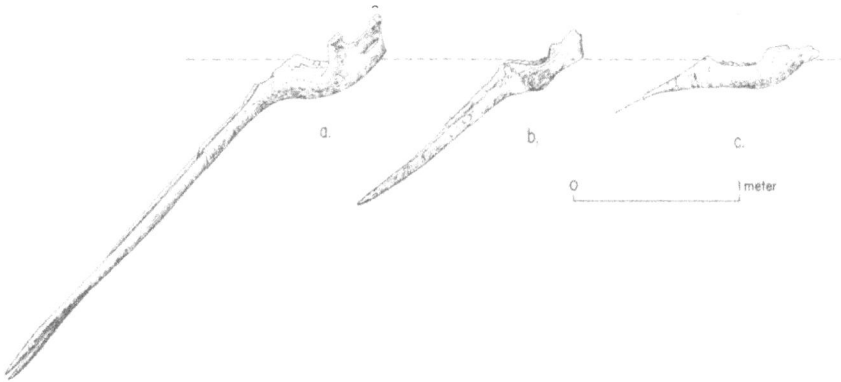

FIGURE 21. Length and angle of symphyses of holotype mandibles of *Stegotetrabelodon* and *Stegodibelodon*.

valleys of the partial M₃ from Saitune Dora (RL09-8) apparently between the P3/4 and the P4/5. On fully erupted molars, buccal posterior columns extend to the P4/5 of the Lothagam M₃ (e.g., KNM LT 359) (Maglio 1973, Pl. 1, Fig. 4), but to the last plate of the Sahabi M₃ (Petrocchi 1954, Pl. V). In addition to differences in molar size and anterior dentition, Maglio (1973) uses the characteristic of the confinement of columns to the anterior end of M₃ of *S. orbus* to distinguish this species from *S. syrticus*, which has posterior columns extending the length of the M₃ (see Character 30, Table 2, Kalb et al., 1992a). In this

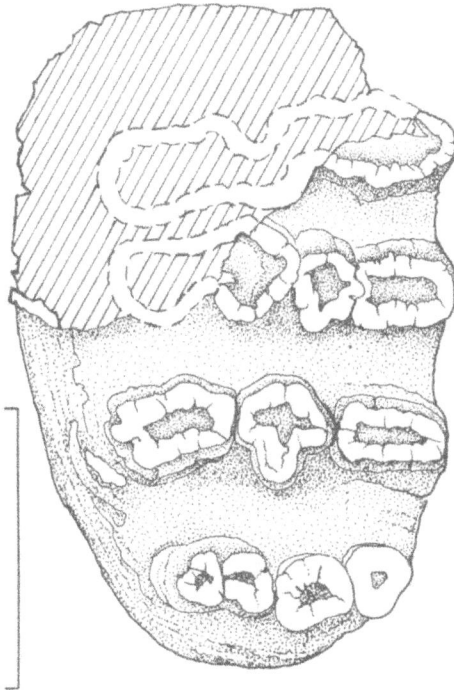

FIGURE 22. Right M²
(photographed, uncollected
specimen), *S. orbus*,
Kuseralee Dora,
Kuseralee Member.

[SCALE = 5 CM]

respect, and in their smaller size, the M^2 and M_3 from Saitune Dora compare more with *S. orbus* (see Maglio 1973, Tables 3, 4).

Intermediate molars (dP4, M1, M2) of the Middle Awash and Lothagam *Stegotetrabelodon* may better distinguish the Sahabi form from the eastern Africa forms. We believe that a pentalophodont M_1 from Lothagam (KNM LT 358) described as *Primelephas gomphotheroides* (Maglio and Ricca 1977, Pl. 1, Fig. 3) is *S. orbus*, which, if so, further helps to distinguish *S. orbus* from *S. syrticus*, which is tetralophodont on both the M_1 and dP_4 (Gaziry 1982, Fig. 2, 1987, Figs. 10 and 11, p. 190; see Kalb et al. 1992a, Appendix I). Both the Sahabi and Lothagam M_1 have broad, open convex-convex enamel loops on the plates. Also, in outline these molars taper anteriorly, a feature Maglio (1973, 19) notes is typical of *Stegotetrabelodon* M_2, with both the M1 and M2 becoming more parallel-sided in true elephants. Tobien (1978a, 196) also notes that the anterior tapering of intermediate molars is a typical "mastodont" feature. In addition, we agree with Gaziry (1987, 197) that an M_2 with concave-concave enamel loops from Lothagam (KNM LT 342) identified as *S. orbus* (Maglio 1973, Pl. II-4) belongs to an early elephant, perhaps *Primelephas* (see below). This specimen is distinct from the convex-convex shaped enamel loops of the holotype M_2 of *S. orbus* (KNM LT 354); in addition, specimen KNM LT 342 has six plates, while the holotype M_2 of *S. orbus* has five plates (Maglio 1970a, Pl. II-6; Maglio 1973, Pl. II-3).

These differences, if true and consistent, are significant because they give *S. syrticus* a plate formula on the lower intermediate molars (dP_4, M_1, M_2) of 4-4-X (no M_2 is as yet described) (Gaziry 1987, 189–190), and a comparable formula for *S. orbus* of X-5-5 (no dP_4 is as yet described). Hence—within the limitations of sample size—*S. syrticus* would be more typically tetralophodont, with *S. orbus* being pentalophodont on the M_1 (but probably not on the dP_4; the dP_3 has three plates) (Maglio and Ricca 1977, Pl. 1, Fig. 8). Both forms are probably pentalophodont on the M_2. Likewise, *S. syrticus* appears to have a plate formula on the upper intermediate molars of X-4-5 (Gaziry 1987, Figs. 15, 16, 1982, Fig. 5), while that for *S. orbus* is reported to be X-5-5 (Maglio and Ricca 1977, 14–16). Since an increase in plate number in increasingly progressive elephantids is the derived condition (e.g., Maglio 1972, 642), these features suggest that *S. orbus* is a more progressive *Stegotetrabelodon* than *S. syrticus* as stated by Maglio (1973), but for additional reasons (see Appendix). Otherwise, we stress that the variation in plate number between species and between individuals of the same species can only be determined by greater sample sizes.

Genus *STEGODIBELODON* Coppens 1972

cf. *STEGODIBELODON SCHNEIDERI* Coppens 1972

(Fig. 23)

Specimen/Locality: L176-1, edentulous mandible, Adu Dora North, upper Adu Member, Adu-Asa Formation (Figs. 2–6, Table 1).

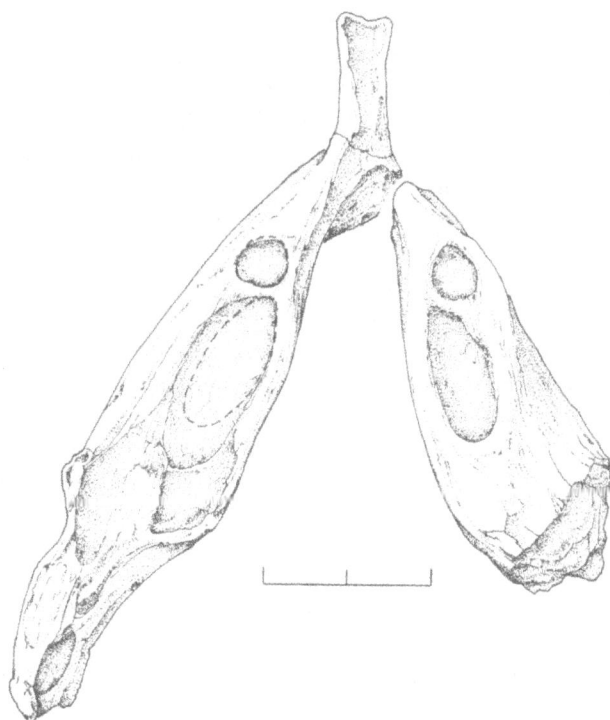

FIGURE 23. **Edentulous mandible (L176-1), cf.** *Stegodibelodon schneideri,* **Adu Dora North, Adu Member.** [SCALE = 20 CM]

Description: L176-1 is an edentulous mandible with a protruding symphysis (Fig. 23). The specimen is complete except for the absence of the coronoid and condyloid processes and vertical ramus of the right side, and the uppermost vertical ramus and condyle of the left side. The horizontal rami have complete alveoli with an anterior and posterior root system (partially filled with matrix). The symphysis is spout-like, short (300 mm), and comprises about 33 percent of the total length of the jaw (ca. 900 mm). It is also sub-horizontal, slender (65 mm minimum and 85 mm maximum width), and solid with no indication of incisors or incisive germ cavities. The dorso-lateral margins of the symphysis are slightly upturned to create a shallow longitudinal trough that broadens anteriorly.

Discussion: L176-1 is similar to the holotype of *Stegodibelodon schneideri* from Menalla, Chad (Coppens 1972; Coppens et al. 1978). Coppens (1972) referred the Chad mandible to the subfamily Stegotetrabelodontinae based on similarities of its M_3 and apparent M^3 (identified from isolated molars of a second individual from Kolinga-1, Chad) with those of *Stegotetrabelodon syrticus* from Sahabi (Petrocchi 1943, 1954) and *S. orbus* from Lothagam (Maglio 1970a, 1973). Coppens et al. (1978) cited the reduced symphysis of the Chad mandible as comparable in a general way to the symphyses of *S. syrticus* and *S. orbus*, particularly the shorter symphysis of *S. orbus* (Figs. 21, 23). Because of the absence of lower incisors (*dibelo-dont*) in the adult Chad form, however, and poorly developed median cleft and weak columns in the (very worn) M3, Coppens (1972) referred the Chad fossils to a new genus, *Stegodibelodon*. Coppens et al. (1978) suggested the lack of lower tusks in *Stegodibelodon* might be due to onto-genetic or sexual variation.

Although the M3 from Menalla are poorly figured (Coppens 1972, Pl. II), and the M³ from Kolinga-I have not been figured at all, we agree with Coppens (1972) that the M3 at least of *Stegodibelodon* are comparable to those of *Stegotetrabelodon*, particularly by the convex-convex enamel loops of lower molars of both genera, a feature not found in true elephants (Appendix, Table 1). However, the elongated and strongly downturned lower symphysis and prominent incisors of *Stegotetrabelodon* remain major distinctions from the brevirostrine mandible of *Stegodibelodon* (Fig. 21) (see Characters 10–13, Table 2, Kalb et al. 1992a). In this respect, Tobien (1978, 167) noted the similarity of the Chad mandible to a man-dible from the Dhok Pathan Formation of the Middle Siwaliks, Pakistan. This specimen was described by Sarwar (1977) as an Asiatic *Stegotetrabelo-don*, *S. maluvalensis*. Both forms have a similar plate number on the M3 (7 and 8 respectively) and lack lower tusks. Primarily because the Pakistan mandible also has four plates on the M2, however, unlike *S. orbus* which has five plates on the M2 (no M2 is available for *S. syrticus*), and has mini-mal cement on the M3, Tobien (1978, 167) suggested the Pakistan man-dible is a progressive form of the genus *Tetralophodon*.

Tobien also suggested that the reduced mandibular symphysis lacking incisors and the abundant cement on the M3 of *Stegodibelodon* place it nearer to early elephants than to *Stegotetrabelodon* (Tobien 1978, 198), while Beden (1979a, 534, 1985) considered the Chad form to be an early loxodont. We feel that the convex-convex enamel loops of M3 of *Stego-dibelodon*, the brevirostrine jaw, and other derived features of the M3 shared with elephants do argue for a form intermediate between that of *Stegotetrabelodon* and early elephants (Appendix). This view is supported by the cladistic models proposed by Tassy and Darlu (1986, Fig. 2) and by Kalb et al. (1992a) (Fig. 7).

Exactly how L176-1 fits into this scheme can only be suggested at this stage because of the absence of dentition; however, L176-1 is similar to *Stegodibelodon* and it is associated stratigraphically with molars similar in their stage of development to those of the Chad mandible. Hence, we would expect L176-1 to be pentalophodont on the M2, and probably the M1, like those reported of the more progressive *Stegotetrabelodon*, *S. orbus*, as discussed above.

STEGODON Falconer 1857
STEGODON cf. *S. KAISENSIS* Hopwood 1939
(Figs. 24, 25)

Specimens/Localities: L89-5a, -5b, juvenile mandible, Saitune Dora, lower Adu-Asa Formation (Asa Member?); L113-1, right M1, L113-2, partial

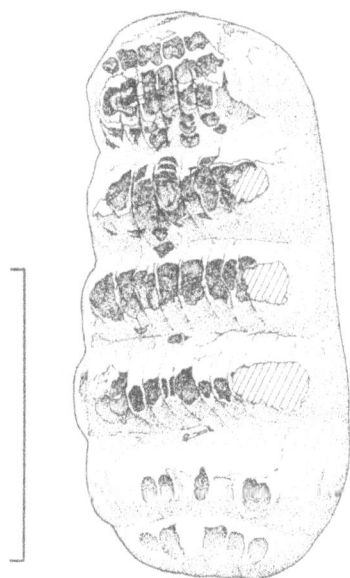

FIGURE 24. Left M_1 (L89 5a),
Stegodon cf. *S. kaisensis*, Saitune Dora,
lower Adu-Asa Formation.
[SCALE = 5 CM]

molar, Adu Dora South, Asa Member, Adu-Asa Formation (Figs. 2–6; Table 1).

Description: L89-5a and -5b is a juvenile mandible in two pieces recovered in association with an array of *Stegotetrabelodon* fossils. The mandible lacks the right ramus, the left coronoid and condyloid processes, and the left vertical ramus. The jaw is brevirostrine, massive and broad. The anterior symphysis is broken, but its base is broad and blunt, and does not

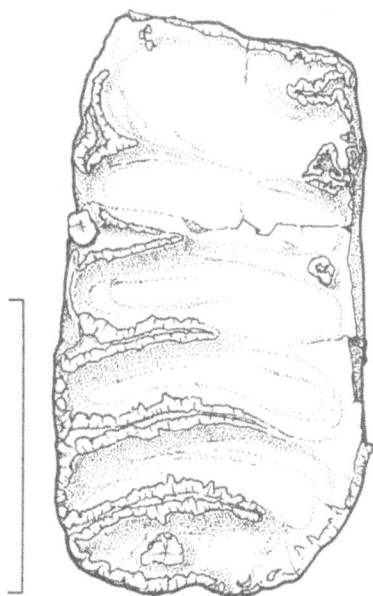

FIGURE 25. Right M_1 (L113-1),
cf. *Stegodon kaisensis*,
Adu Dora South, Asa Member.
[SCALE = 5 CM]

appear to have been elongated. L89-5b contains a complete but very worn right dP_4 and a nearly complete M_1, while L89-5a contains a crushed left dP_4 and a complete M_1 (Fig. 24). The right dP_4 has four plates (L $\approx$ 48 mm, W $\approx$ 36 mm) worn to their base. The M_1 have five plates with pronounced anterior and posterior platelets, with very modest anterior wear. The left M_1 has a length (101 mm) twice the width (49 mm), an estimated height and hypsodonty of 42 mm and 86, and a lamellar frequency of three. The M_1 tapers anteriorly with the width being greatest (49 mm) on the fourth plate (P4); the width is 40 mm on the P1. Plates are subdivided into 10–11 tiny, elongated mammillae separated by fine, longitudinal grooves. The mammillae are modestly flattened and nearly equal in height. No median cleft is present. Medial columns are present in the anterior transverse valleys. The transverse crests and mammillae are subparallel although more clearly arranged in a shallow convex-convex shape at the posterior end of the molar. The valleys are V-shaped and partially filled with cement. The plate faces are also partially covered with cement.

L113-1 is an extremely worn molar that appears to be a right M_1 (Fig. 25). The anterior root is broken while the posterior root is well developed and nearly complete. Much of the anterior end and buccal side of the molar is worn beneath the crown. L113-1 is similar in size and shape to L89-5a, with an identical length of 101 mm, a lamellar frequency of three, but a greater width on the P4 (57 mm) and P1 (54 mm). Like L89-5a, L113-1 has five plates and prominent anterior and posterior platelets. The P3-5 and posterior platelet are convex-convex, while the anterior platelet and P1-2 show the remnant of concave-concave curvature, particularly at the lateral margins. Plates are tightly compressed (in extreme wear) with enamel loops touching nearly the width of the molar. Columns are present in the valley between the P2/3 on either side at the lateral margin. The enamel is thin, very tightly crenulated, and scallop-like with fine longitudinal grooves.

L113-2 is an extremely worn molar fragment with root from the same individual as L113-1. It consists of 2½ partial convex-convex plates the same size as those of L113-1; they are worn to the very base of the crown with virtually no enamel remaining. The root is not as developed as the posterior root of L113-1 and appears to represent the anterior end of the tooth. The direction and wear of the remnant ridges suggest that it is a lingual fragment, perhaps a left M_2. The wear of L113-1 also indicates that the M_2 were partially erupted and well worn anteriorly.

Discussion: Distinctive features of the M_1 of L89-5 are their numerous mammillae and associated superficial, longitudinal grooves, and deep V-shaped valleys filled with cement, features characteristic of *Stegodon*. This genus was very prominent in Asia in the Plio-Pleistocene and developed similarly to the African elephants with respect to its crania, dentition, and short jaws (Osborn 1942; Saegusa 1987).

In Africa, two species of *Stegodon* have been reported, *S. syrticus* from

Sahabi (Petrocchi 1943, 1954) and *S. kaisensis* from Kaiso and elsewhere in Uganda (Hopwood 1939; MacInnes 1942; Cooke and Coryndon 1970; Sanders 1990), Chad (Coppens 1965, 340; see Maglio 1973, 20), and Ethiopia's Omo Valley (Beden 1976, 1987b) (Fig. 3). There are no M_1 or dP_4 from these localities that are comparable to L89-5, although figured partial molars (M15171 and M26310), which may be M1 from Uganda (Cooke and Coryndon 1970, Pl. 2C–E) and upper Member B of the Shungura Formation (Beden 1976, Fig. 2B) (Fig. 3), are similar morphologically. Whereas the number of mammillae in the (worn) Uganda specimens number 6–7, those in the (unworn) Shungura molars number 10–11, like L89-5a and an unworn M^2 (M15407) from Kazinga, Uganda (MacInnes 1942, Pl. VII-7). In 1942, MacInnes designated the latter the holotype of *Stegodon fuchsi*, but the Kazinga M^2 and a much abraded M^1 from the same individual were later judged to be identical to *S. kaisensis* described (but not figured) by Hopwood in 1939 (Arambourg 1948, 305; Coppens 1965, 340, Cooke and Coryndon 1970). Cooke and Coryndon (1970, 122) note substantial differences in apparent morphology between the Kazinga M^2 and M^1, which they attribute to wear. They also describe the M^1 (M15408) as inseparable morphologically from the holotype (M15170) of *S. kaisensis* from Kaiso, which they identify as an M_1, although unfortunately the Kazinga M^1 has not been figured.

The plate number (five) of L89-5a, an M_1, is low for Asian *Stegodon* (Osborn 1942, 809, 854) and probably low for the *Stegodon* from Kazinga (MacInnes 1942, Pl. VII-7; Cooke and Coryndon 1970, Table IV). Cooke and Coryndon (1970, 121, Pl. 2A) estimate the plate number of the *S. kaisensis* holotype (M15170) to be seven on the partial but reconstructed molar, believed to be an M_1. We note, however, that the estimated length of this molar (≈ 200 mm) is near that of the M^2 from Kazinga (193 mm) and twice the length (101 mm) of the Saitune Dora M_1.

The plate number of L89-5a is consistent with *Stegotetrabelodon*, probably *S. orbus* (see below); also, L89-5a possesses anterior intra-valley columns, lacking in described species of *Stegodon*. Otherwise, the brevirostrine jaw of L89-5 is unlike that expected in a juvenile *Stegotetrabelodon* mandible, although it is possible that with preparation and recovery of more of the specimen L89-5 may prove to be less brevirostrine than is apparent. We believe a juvenile mandible from Lothagam described by Maglio (1970a, 1973) and Maglio and Ricca (1978) as *Primelephas* is in fact *Stegotetrabelodon* (Kalb et al. 1992a, Appendix I, *Primelephas*). This specimen is a more youthful individual than L89-5, with well-worn M_1, and has an extended mandibular symphysis with a small incisor. Gaziry (1987, 189, Fig. 9) points out the massive aspect of a partial juvenile hemimandible from Sahabi that has a dP_4 and an unerupted M_1. The dP_4 has anterior intra-valley columns, like L89-5a, and is subdivided into 7–8 mammillae-like apices, separated by fine longitudinal grooves. (The dP_4 are too worn or abraded to show accessory features.) A more prominent groove, or modest cleft, occurs along the medial axis of the Sahabi dP_4, that is also lacking in the Saitune Dora M_1, but which is present anteriorally on the M² from Kazinga and on the M³ of *Stegodon syrticus* from Sahabi (MacInnes 1942, Pl. VII-7; Petrocchi 1943, Figs. 70–71, 1953, Pl. VII).

As discussed, L113-1 is similar in shape, size, and plate number to L89-5a; it also has anterior intra-valley columns although distinctly lateral in position (Figs. 24, 25). Like *Stegodon*, the enamel is tightly crenulated and scallop-like with numerous fine longitudinal grooves. The convex-convex plates of L113-1 are not typical of lower molars of *Stegodon*, which tend to be straight or display a very shallow curvature. Such could indicate a closer comparison with lower molars of *Stegotetrabelodon* or *Stegodibelodon*. On the other hand, L113-1 is of a very early age (probably 5–6 m.y.) and the specimen is extremely worn. With wear, it is likely that the posterior plates of L89-5a would show a more prominent convexity.

Overall, L89-5 and L113-1 bear features similar to *Stegodon* and *Stegotetrabelodon* and *Stegodibelodon*. Characters found in *Stegodon* are clearly present in the intermediate, unworn molars of *Stegotetrabelodon*, such as the dP₄ and M¹ from Sahabi (Gaziry 1987, Figs. 10 and 16; 1982, Fig. 5 – we believe the molar identified as an M² is an M¹). Otherwise, L89-5a may best be regarded as an early *Stegodon* similar to *S. kaisensis*, but with anterior intra-valley columns that suggest a somewhat earlier form. Since it is likely that more of L89-5 and L113-1 can be recovered, possibly including cranial material, further identification should await this eventuality. At this stage we refer to L89-5 as *Stegodon* cf. *S. kaisensis* and L113-1 as cf. *S. kaisensis*.

Subfamily *ELEPHANTINAE* Gray 1821
Genus *PRIMELEPHAS* Maglio 1970a
PRIMELEPHAS GOMPHOTHEROIDES Maglio 1970a
(Figs. 26, 27)

Specimens/Localities: L110-1, left M², Dofa, Asa Member; L211-2, right M², Kuseralee Dora, Kuseralee Member, Adu-Asa Formation (Figs. 2–6, Table 1).

Description: L110-1 is a moderately worn, incomplete left M² with a partial root, 2½ posterior plates, and a heel (Fig. 26). The molar is 74 mm in length, 42 mm in height, low crowned (HI ≈ 56), and has thick enamel (ET = 3–6 mm). The plates are nearly parallel but with a very shallow convex-convex shape, widely spaced (LF ≈ 4.5) and full, compressed loops. L110-1 is widest (75 mm) at the last full plate (probably the P5) and narrows slightly anteriorly. Valleys are broadly V-shaped and partially filled with cement. No median cleft is present but weak, longitudinal grooves divide the occlusal surface, indicating that the unworn molar probably had six apical digitations on the full plates. Four digitations are present on the posterior heel. Also, no intra-valley columns are present.

L211-2 is a right M², largely unworn and nearly complete (Fig. 27). Five full plates, a modest anterior platelet, and a prominent heel are present; the root is absent. Only the P5 is partially broken on the lingual margin, and the occlusal surface of the molar is partially abraded

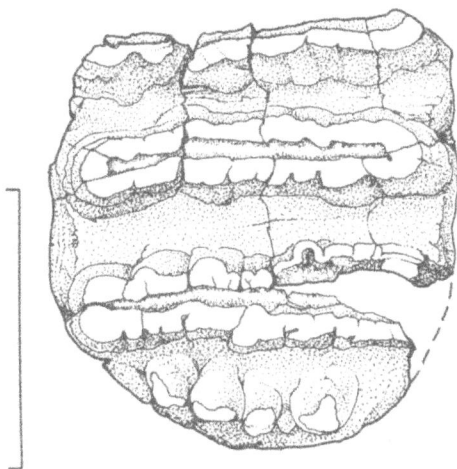

FIGURE 26. Left M^2 (L110F-1),
Primelephas gomphotheroides,
Dofa, Asa Member.
[SCALE = 5 CM]

and chipped, revealing five to six digitations on each plate. Cement
nearly fills the valleys and covers most of the plate faces and the heel.
A median column is exposed just beneath the cement posterior to the
P1. The column is off center nearest to the lingual (pretrite) side of
the molar. L211-2 is proportionally very similar to L110-1, with a length

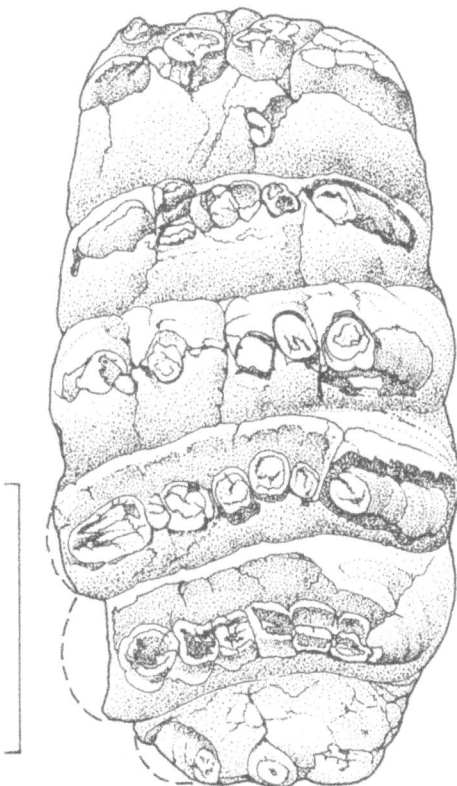

FIGURE 27. Right M^2 (L211-2),
P. gomphotheroides,
Kuseralee Dora, Kuseralee Member.
[SCALE = 5 CM]

of 78 mm at the P3, and a total length of 149 mm. The maximum width
(74 mm) and lamellar frequency (4.5) of L211-2 are also similar to that of
L110-1. The hypsodonty (64) is higher than that of L110-1 ($\approx$56),
although L211-1 is nearly unworn. The valleys of L211-2 are broadly
V-shaped but are slightly more compressed than those of L110-1. The
plates of L211-2 taper anteriorly: the width at the P1 is 65 mm, while the
width at the P4 is 74 mm. The P5 and P4 are clearly convex-convex, while
the remaining plates are more parallel.

Discussion: L110-1 and L211-2 show the characteristic features of M^2 of
Primelephas gomphotheroides, an early elephant initially described by Maglio
(1970a) as the basal genus and species from which later "true elephants"
could have derived. L110-1 and L211-1 are very similar, although smaller
than a left M^2 of *P. gomphotheroides* from Lothagam-1 (KNM LT 358)
(Maglio 1973, Pl. III-3) and a fragmentary right M^2 of the same species
from Lukeino-A (KNM LU 718) (Tassy 1986, Pl. XIV-1, -2). The latter M^2
and L211-2 all have five plates and a prominent posterior heel; also, they
have anterior lingual columns posterior to concave-concave enamel loops.
L211-1 is similar to the Lukeino-A right M^2, which also has an anterior
medial column just on the buccal (pretrite) side of the molar.

   Primelephas upper molars differ generally from those of *Stegotetrabelo-*
don by having more apical digitations (or apices that are divided by longitudinal grooves), more compressed plates, broader transverse valleys,
greater cement development, and an absence of median clefts, or the
presence of median clefts that are weak and confined to the anterior end
of the molar (Appendix, Table 1). All but the last feature are present on
L110-1 and L211-2. Two uncollected (but photographed M_3) from the
Kuseralee Member are also morphologically similar to *P. gomphotheroides*
by having 8–9 plates, low lamellar frequency (3.5–4), thick enamel (4–5),
and low hypsodonty (62–67).

   The above M^2 compare with M_2 from Lothagam-1. Specimen KNM
LT 342 is a left M_2 (Maglio 1973, Pl. II-4) and "54–67K" is a right M_2
(number and photo provided by V. Maglio). Like the M^2, the M_2 have
compressed concave-concave plates; unlike the M^2, the posterior columns
of the M_3 extend to the posterior half of the molar and are present on
the buccal side.

Genus *LOXODONTA*
F. Cuvier and Geoffroy Saint-Hilaire 1825

Loxodonts have been recovered throughout much of the Middle Awash
Pliocene from the Sagantole, Hadar and Matabaietu Formations (Figs. 4–6).
The two known loxodont lineages are represented by the earliest recog-
nized species from each, *Loxodonta adaurora* and *L. exoptata* (Beden 1985,
Fig. 2) (Fig. 7). Whereas the former is confined to the middle and upper
Pliocene in the Afar, like elsewhere in Africa, the lineage represented by
L. exoptata–L. atlantica–L. africana apparently originated in the late Miocene

with an as yet un-named early loxodont from Lukeino-A described by Tassy (1986, 115).

Molars of the two living elephant genera, the Asiatic *Elephas* and the African *Loxodonta*, were originally distinguished by Frédéric Cuvier on the basis of parallel-like enamel loops on worn plates of *Elephas*, and oblique-sided ("lox" in Greek) or lozenge-shaped enamel loops in *Loxodonta africana* (Osborn, 1942, 1174). The distinctive shape of plates of the *L. africana* lineage has long allowed its representatives to be recognized in the African fossil record. Apparently, the first reported fossil loxodonts — now referred to as *L. atlantica* — were described from opposite ends of the continent: from North Africa by Pomel in 1879 and from South Africa 50 years later by Dart (1929), who may have been the first to apply the genus *Loxodonta* to fossil elephants (Osborn 1942, 1287). In 1929, Dart (1929, 730) suggested that southern Africa may be "the evolutionary home of the modern African elephant."

Hopwood (1936) was apparently the first to recognize loxodont-like elephants from East Africa, from Laetoli, Tanzania (Kent 1941; Beden 1987a) (Fig. 3). Coppens (1965) later referred the Laetoli elephants to the genus *Loxodonta*. Beden (1987a, 259–260) assigned the species, *L. exoptata*, to these elephants, a name derived from *Archidiskodon exoptatus* (Dietrich 1941). The early elephant from Lukeino-A, described by Tassy (1986) as "cf. *Loxodonta*," appears to be ancestral to *L. exoptata* (Kalb et al. 1992a, Appendix I). Maglio (1969, 1970a) recognized a second loxodont lineage in Africa, represented by the species, *L. adaurora*, which he described from the Kanapoi, Lothagam (Unit-3) and Ekora, Kenya (Maglio 1970a, 1973). Beden (1979a, 1983) later distinguished two subspecies of *L. adaurora*, *L. a. adaurora*, and *L. a. kararae*.

LOXODONTA ADAURORA Maglio 1970a
(Figs. 28, 29)

Specimens/Localities: L151-1, left M_2, Wee-ee Dora, Aramis Member(?), Sagantole Formation; L123A-1a, left M_2(?), Wadayemero Dora, upper Sagantole Formation (Figs. 2–4, 6, Table 1).

Description: L151-1 is a left M_2 in a jaw fragment (Fig. 28). The tooth sits low and fully forward in the lower jaw. The horizontal ramus is broken just anterior to the M_2 at the mental foramen, slightly forward of the last plate, and is fully parallel with respect to the molar crown. The jaw flares on the buccal side at the base of the vertical ramus.

The tooth is moderately worn, broken at the anterior end, and chipped on the posterior lingual side. Six plates and a posterior platelet are present. The molar length is 220 mm with a maximum width of 101 mm in the mid-region. The width is uniform but tapers prominently on the last two plates. Plates are widest at their base and are widely spaced (LF = 4). The height and hypsodonty (above the jaw) are 44 mm and 43 respectively and the enamel is thick (3–5 mm) and even.

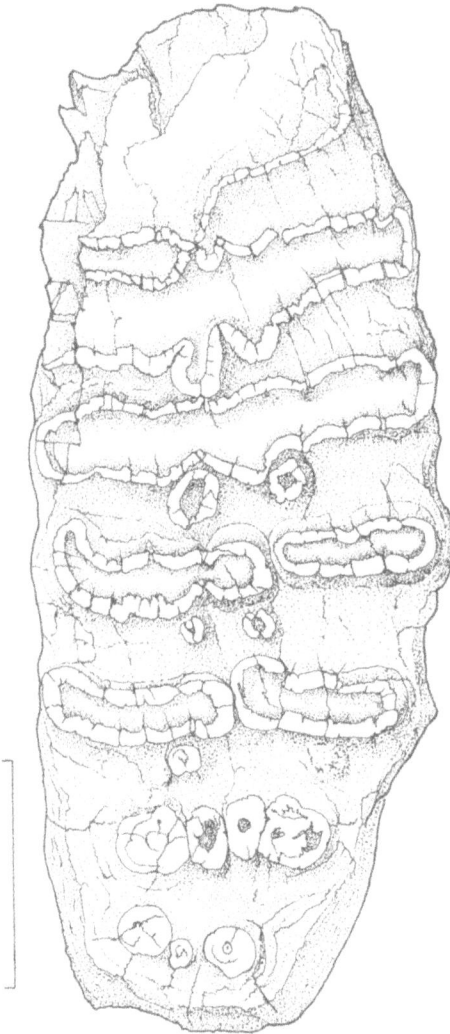

FIGURE 28. Left M₂ (L151-1),
Loxodonta adaurora, **Wee-ee,
Sagantole Formation.**

[SCALE = 5 CM]

The first three plates have enamel loops that are expanded medially. The first plate is only partially intact due to wear and breakage; a rounded, prominent posterior medial loop is present. The second plate possesses two posterior medial loops that are broad and lobate from incorporation of paired buccal and lingual posterior columns. This plate shows some anterior medial expansion due to longitudinal offset of the half-plates. The anterior face of the plate is contiguous to the posterior loop of the first plate. The third plate is indented posteriorly between two isolated, medial columns. The fourth and fifth plates are divided into hemi-loops with the plates separated from each other by paired medial columns. Similar columns are present posterior to the fifth plate. The distance between pairs of columns increases posteriorly. The last full plate is divided into four apical digitations; the posterior heel consists of three apical digitations. The overall aspect of the crown surface of the plates

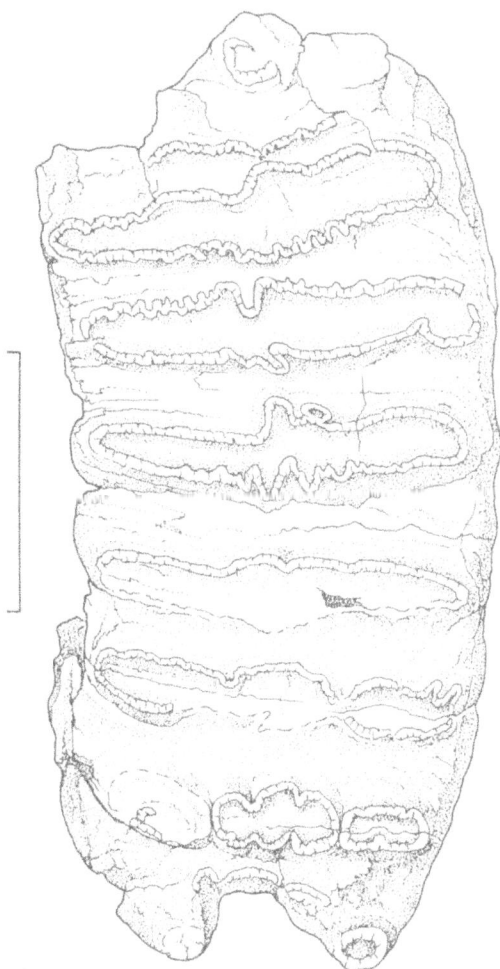

FIGURE 29. Left M$_2$ (?)(L123A-1a),
L. adaurora, Wadayemero,
upper Sagantole Formation.
[SCALE = 5 CM]

is an elongated rectangular appearance with opposing faces of the plates
having a compressed, shallow concave-concave shape, particularly at the
buccal margin of the posterior plates.

L123A-1a, like L151-1, is a partial left lower molar, perhaps an M$_2$,
that is moderately worn (Fig. 29). It has a strong anterior root, six full
plates, and broken plates at either end. The width (92 mm) is greatest
on the second full plate and remains nearly uniform posteriorly; the
height is 78 mm. The hypsodonty is 85 but was probably closer to 95 on
the complete molar. The length is 96 mm and the lamellar frequency is
4.2. The enamel is thin (2–2.5 mm) and tightly folded medially.

The anterior three full plates of L123A-1a possess complete enamel
loops that show modest expansion medially, but otherwise have a very
shallow, compressed concave-concave shape with rounded lateral margins. The first full plate (probably the P2 or P3 of the complete molar)
has two modest, rounded anterior medial folds. The second plate has
two pointed anterior medial folds, a pronounced sinus, and a single

asymmetrical, posterior medial loop. The third plate has a single, anterior medial loop contiguous to a small, adjacent column, and two pointed, posterior loops. The fourth plate is partially obscured by matrix but it appears to have a broad posterior fold. The fifth and sixth plates are segmented resulting from only moderate wear, revealing 7–8 apical digitations on each plate.

Discussion: The M_2 from Wee-ee (L151-1) appears to be an early *L. adaurora* indicated by shallow concave-concave compressed plates and paired posterior columns. These features are morphologically consistent with the type M_3 of *L. adaurora* from Kanapoi (Maglio 1970a, 1973). Specimen KNM KP-385 has paired columns posterior to the plates in the mid-region of the molars. The columns are not apparent on the worn anterior and unworn posterior portions of the M_3 (indicating their confinement to the mid-height region of the molar). The columns are more fused to the half-plates of the Kanapoi M_3 than are the columns of L151-1, and the lingual (posttrite) columns are poorly developed. The isolated prominent paired columns of L151-1 extending to the posterior end of the M_2 indicate a form that is somewhat more primitive than the Kanapoi loxodont. In this regard, it is likely that the lower Wee-ee beds (3.8 ≤ 4.1 m.y.) are modestly older than the Kanapoi beds (Haileab and Brown 1992) (Table 1, Figs. 3–4).

Partially erupted matching M_3 (FS 160/17-17a and FS160/18-18A, numbers and photos from V. Maglio) from East Turkana also appear to be *L. adaurora.* These specimens come from the "Kubi Algi Formation," deposits which have since been incorporated into the lower Koobi Fora Formation (Brown and Feibel 1986; Beden 1983, 47) (Fig. 3). These M_3, however, have paired posterior columns confined to the anterior end of the molars. In this regard, Beden (1983) has described a more progressive grade of *L. adaurora* from the middle Koobi Fora Formation. He refers to this form as the subspecies *L. a. kararae,* and those from the lower Koobi Fora and Kanapoi beds as *L. a. adaurora.* He also reports that *L. a. adaurora* is present in the middle Hadar Formation (Beden 1985, Table 1) (Fig. 6a). Beden distinguishes these forms on skull and molar characteristics. He describes the anterior and posterior plate faces of *L. a. kararae* as being less convergent than those of *L. a. adaurora,* meaning that there have been further incorporation and medial alignment of accessory features with the increased compression of plates. (Unfortunately, the figured specimens of *L. a. kararae* have little wear that reveals the configuration of the enamel loops with respect to column development.) Using Beden's criteria and metric data (Beden 1983, Tables 3.4 and 3.7), L151-1 would be referred to as *L. a. adaurora.* L123A-1a is about 10 percent smaller in size than L151-1 with a corresponding increase in lamellar frequency; also, the hypsodonty is greater and the enamel thinner and distinctly more folded medially. Thus, L123A-1a would be more progressive than L151-1 but not as progressive as *L. a. kararae.*

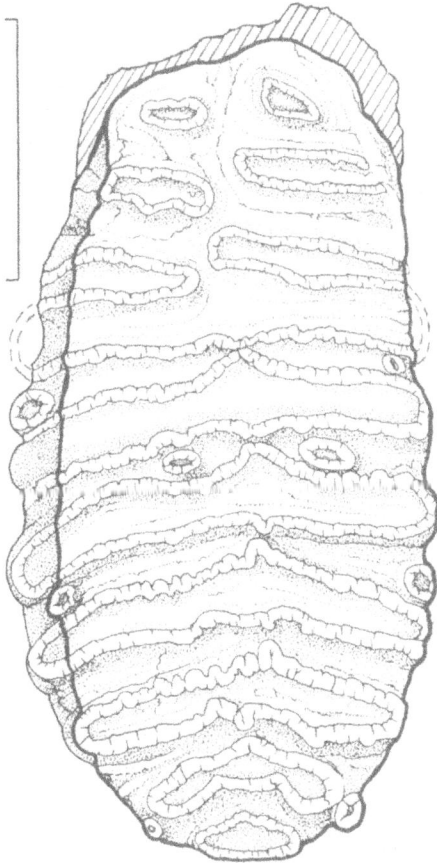

FIGURE 30. Right M² (L77-1),
L. exoptata, Matabaietu,
Matabaietu Formation.

[SCALE = 5 CM]

LOXODONTA EXOPTATA (Dietrich) 1941
(Figs. 30, 31)

Specimen/Locality: L77-1, right M², and L4-12, partial upper molar, Matabaietu Dora, Matabaietu Formation (Figs. 2-6, Table 1).

Description: L77-1 is a right M² in a maxilla fragment (Fig. 30) consisting of portions of the interalveolar crest and the ptergygoid process nearest the molar. The M² is complete with eight plates and a small posterior heel. Only part of the anterior root is missing; the root that is present is strong and transverse. The tooth is well worn the length of the molar leaving the lateral ends of some of the plates on the occlusal surface truncated at the margins of the molar. The M² is 167 mm long and distinctively ovoid-shaped: it is widest in the middle, 83 mm, and tapers strongly at both ends. Plates flare outward from the base of the molar giving a maximum width at the crown surface. The crown height is 40 mm, the hypsodonty is 48 (on a very worn molar), and plates are moderately spaced (LF = 5).

Anterior wear reveals the "expanding loxodont sinus" referred to by Osborn (1942, Fig. 1057) resulting in three, offset pairs of enamel islands that become increasingly elongated posteriorly. Opposing faces of the remaining plates converge near the midline just off center on the lingual side of the molar. The anterior plates merge in the transverse valleys and the remaining plates are contiguous. Medial folds are simple and obtuse, becoming compressed anteriorly. The overall aspect of the full plates is a flattened, convex-convex shape in the mid-region, becoming more convex posteriorly.

The enamel increases in thickness posteriorly (ranging from 2–4 mm) with a similar increase in folding. A particular feature of L77-1 is pairs of small, oval lateral columns or tubercles between the P3/4, P4/5, and P5/6 (Fig. 30). Columns are at the lateral margins between the P3/4 and P5/6 and near the midline between the P4/5. Columns are also aligned laterally with the P8.

L4-12 consists of the posterior 2½ plates and heel of an upper molar (Fig. 31). The specimen is 70 mm long and 68 mm wide. The full plates are convex-convex, expanded medially and nearly symmetrically, and increasingly compressed laterally. The plate faces are nearly touching near their midlines, giving the plates a single "propeller" shape. The enamel is thick (3–5 mm) and tightly folded in the mid-region of the posterior plate faces. The plate faces, particularly those anteriorly, slope markedly posteriorly, which gives the appearance that the enamel is much thicker than it actually is (Fig. 31).

Discussion: The compressed convex-shape and convergence of the symmetrical, opposing plate faces of L77-1, compared to L151-1 and L123A-1a, are distinctive of well-worn molars of L. exoptata (Beden 1983, 1987a). Molars of this species are distinguished from later loxodonts (L. atlantica and L. africana) by their lower plate number and their specialized enamel

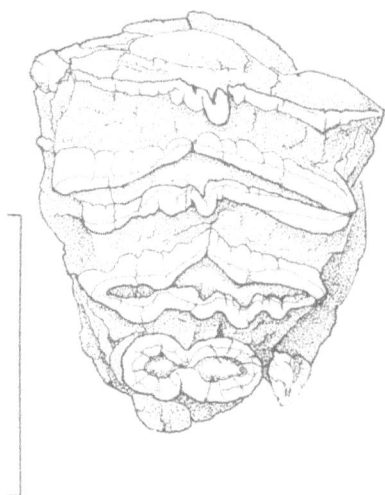

FIGURE 31. Partial upper molar (L4-12), *L. exoptata*, Matabaietu, Matabaietu Formation.
[SCALE = 5 CM]

loops, which are more evenly compressed laterally with more localized axial expansion.

L77-1 is similar in size and morphology to M² of *L. exoptata* from the Laetolil Beds, Tanzania (Beden 1987a, Pl. 8.3, Figs. 18, 23, 1979a, Fig. 64A) and the lower Koobi Fora Formation (Beden 1983, Fig. 3.9C; Brown and Feibel 1986) (Fig. 3). The plate morphology is also consistent with that of other cheek teeth from the Laetolil and Koobi Fora beds (Maglio 1969, Pl. II-6; Beden 1979a, Fig. 63, 1983, Fig. 3.9A,B) and from Member D of the Shungura Formation (Beden 1979a, Fig. 66). We cannot explain the distinctive twin, lateral columns present in L77-1, however, which appear to distinguish this molar from other known molars of *L. exoptata*. Only a single M³ attributable to this species from Laetoli has lateral, anterior columns between plates, but these are single columns (Maglio 1969, Pl. II-6; Beden 1979a, Fig. 63). L77-1 also differs slightly from previously described (and similarly worn) molars of *L. exoptata* by having plates that are more compressed, particularly when comparing L77-1 with molars of *L. exoptata* from the upper Laetolil Beds (Beden 1987a). Unfortunately, *L. exoptata* identified from the Denen Dora Member at Hadar (Beden 1985, Table 1) remains undescribed and unfigured, as are molars (e.g., AL105-7) which we believe may belong to this same species from Amado, a site 45 km northwest of Hadar (Kalb and Peak 1975) (Figs. 1 and 5). In addition, skull material belonging to L77-1 is present at the Matabaietu site and awaits recovery and description.

The propeller-shaped plates of L4-12 are also typical of *L. exoptata* (see Maglio 1969, Pl. II, Fig. 6; Beden 1987a, Pl. 8.3, Fig. 1, 1983, Fig. 3.9, 1987b, Fig. 7).

Genus *MAMMUTHUS* Burnet 1830
MAMMUTHUS SUBPLANIFRONS (Osborn) 1928
(Fig. 32, 33)

Specimens/Localities: L27-1a, left M₃, L27-1b, partial left M³, L27-1c, M2 fragment, eastern Wee-ee Dora, Aramis Member(?), Sagantole Formation; L210-1, partial right M₃, Kuseralee Dora, Kuseralee Member, Adu-Asa Formation (Figs. 2–6, Table 1).

Description: L27-1a is a complete left M₃; much of this individual remains at the locality. L27-1a possesses eight widely spaced plates (LF = 3.5) with prominent platelets at either end (Fig. 32). The root is completely absent. The molar is large (L = 245 mm, W = 101 mm) with a relatively low crown height (HI = 76); the enamel is thick (ET = 4–4.5 mm) and unfolded. Only the P1-3 are worn; the anterior end is worn to about half the height of the molar. Valleys between unworn plates are nearly filled with cement. The plates are concave-concave in shape. The P1 consists of two half-loops widely separated by a median cleft and possessing a prominent posterior column. The P2 consists of two half-loops that are nearly touching, while the P3 consists of five apical digitations. The P1-7 are nearly uniform in width, while the P8 and heel taper sharply. The

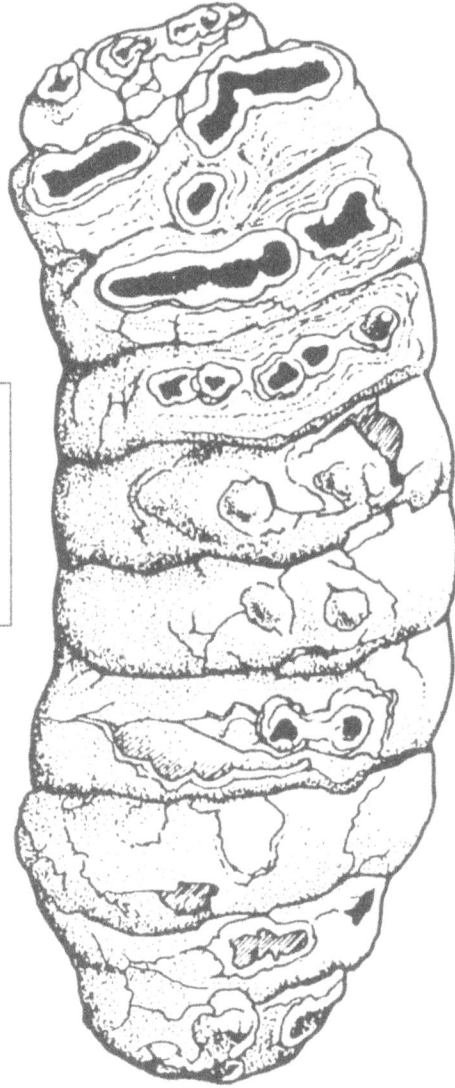

FIGURE 32. Left M$_3$ (L27-1a),
Mammuthus subplanifrons,
Wee-ee, Sagantole Formation.
[SCALE = 5 CM]

plates are also widest at the occusal surface, tapering at the base. The molar is silicified and unusually well preserved. Twelve to 13 concentric growth layers of dentine are revealed at the anterior end of the molar (between enamel loops) and on the underside (base) of the molar where the roots are sheared away.

L27-1b appears to be a partial left M^3 from the same individual as L27-1a. L27-1b consists of the first five plates of a molar that probably had seven full plates (Mebrate and Kalb 1981, Fig. 2). The root is absent. The first plate is partially broken. Wear is similar to that of L27-1a and is greatest on the buccal side. The first plate is very irregular but roughly concave-concave in shape with a prominent posterior medial fold. The second plate is only partially worn but the lateral margins taper in a

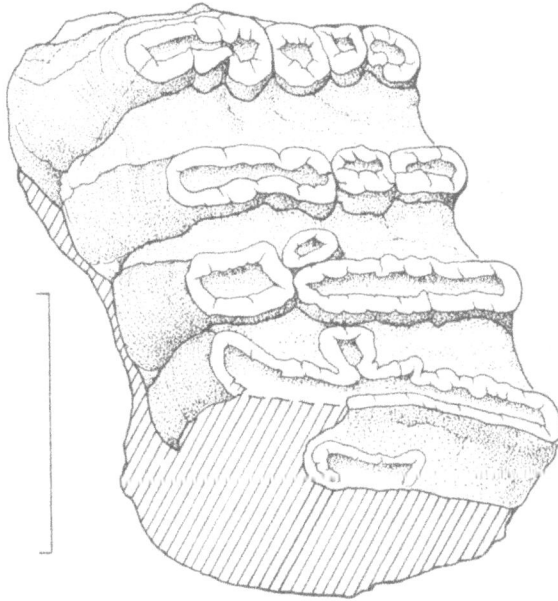

FIGURE 33.   Right M₃ (L210-1), cf. *M. subplanifrons*, Kuseralee Dora, Kuseralee Member.
[SCALE = 5 CM]

convex-convex pattern. Six apical digitations are present on the third plate. Like L27-1a, the plates of L27-1b are widely spaced (LF = 3.5) and broad (W = 102 mm) but have a higher hypsodonty (HI = 89).

L27-1c is an M2 fragment, either a left M_2 or a right M^2, with a partial root, from the same individual as L27-1a. It consists of five partial plates of a molar that probably had six plates, perhaps seven. The tooth is broken at either end and longitudinally, leaving only the buccal half of the plates. The tooth is heavily worn, revealing thick, broad lobate loops extending the full width of the molar, which nearly touch in the center. The anterior two plates are concave-concave in shape, and the third plate is convex-convex; no medial folds are preserved. The anterior end is especially worn. The limited anterior wear of L27-1a and -1b suggests that L27-1c was fully erupted and may have lost one plate.

L210-1 is a partial, moderately worn molar, probably a right M_3, that is broken at both ends (Fig. 33). Four nearly complete anterior plates (L = 133 mm) are present that may represent the P2-5 of a young adult; the complete molar probably had 8–9 plates. The plates have a very shallow convex-convex shape, particularly at the lateral margins of the posterior two plates. The anteriormost plate forms a complete, compressed loop with a column fused to the posterior face. A column is also fused to the posterior surface of the next plate. Superficial grooves partially divide the posterior plates into half-loops on the lingual side and 2–3 apical digitations on the buccal side; 5–6 digitations were present on the unworn molar. The plates are very broad, parallel-sided, uniform (W = 90–96 mm), and widely spaced (LF = 4). The tooth is also low crowned (H = 60–64) with a low hypsodonty (HI = ca. 60) and thick enamel (3–4 mm). Valleys are broadly V-shaped and nearly filled with cement.

Discussion: L27-1a is very similar in morphology and wear to matching M3 of the same individual (SAM-L 12723B and SAM-L 12723C) from the Varswater Formation, Langebaanweg, as we have discussed elsewhere (Mebrate and Kalb 1981) (Fig. 3). The South African elephant is referred to as the earliest known mammoth, *Mammuthus subplanifrons* (Maglio 1973, Pl. XV-1; Hendey 1978, 8–9; Maglio and Hendey, 1970, Pl. II). The Langebaanweg specimens are the only M3 of this species associated with a jaw and for this reason can be considered to be the best-known specimens of *M. subplanifrons*. Both the Awash and the Langebaanweg M3 are broad, uniform molars with abundant cement, even enamel and similar hypsodonty (HI = 76 and 79 respectively); also, both M3 have a median cleft on the P1. The size of the Langebaanweg M3 (L = 320 mm, W = 110 mm) is significantly greater than that of L27-1a (L = 245 mm, W = 101 mm); the lamellar frequency is also lower (3.0 versus 3.5). In addition, the Langebaanweg M3 have nine plates instead of eight and an additional apical digitation per plate, which are derived features not found in the Wee-ee M3.

Like the Langebaanweg M3, L27-1a also has a prominent column posterior to the enamel loops of the P1. The matching Langebaanweg M3 also have a second much reduced lateral column posterior to the P1, as well as single columns posterior to the P2 and P3. With a greater sample size, the presence of single posterior columns posterior to the enamel loops of anterior plates of lower molars may prove to be a distinguishing characteristic of early *Mammuthus*, when combined with the compressed, concave-concave shape of enamel loops of the lower molars. The enamel loops of worn lower molars of *M. subplanifrons* have a more rectilinear shape with concavity being more subtle and more expressed at the lateral margins, particularly on the South African M3.

L27-1b, the partial M³, is also consistent with *M. subplanifrons*; it's hypsodonty (89) is greater than that of *Stegotetrabelodon* (68–75) or *Primelephas* (57–64), but lower than that of *Elephas ekorensis* (109–114) (Maglio 1973; Beden 1979a). Although L27-1c appears to be a partial M2, it is similar in morphology to well-worn M3 from Kanam East, Kenya, which Maglio (1973, Pl. XV-3, -4) refers to as *M. subplanifrons*. Like the Kanam molars, L27-1c has broad, lobate open loops that are nearly parallel-sided, giving them an overall elongated and rectangular shape.

An interesting feature of L27-1a are the 12–13 annual concentric layers of dentine revealed on the underside of the molar and partially visible in the valleys between plates at the worn anterior end of the molar (Fig. 32). Based on aging criteria of the extant *L. africana* (Laws 1966; Sikes 1971), we can roughly estimate the Wee-ee elephant to have been approximately 30–35 years old. Dentine formation on M3 of North American mastodonts typically begins between the ages of 15–20 years and continues until the animal is between 25–30 years old (Dan Fisher, University of

Michigan, pers. com., 1992). By analogy, we can suggest that the dentine growth layers in the Wee-ee M_3 began forming during the latter half of the individual's life and may have ceased forming shortly before or at the time of death.

Whereas *M. subplanifrons* is the earliest recognized mammoth, a more derived form is reported from the Sidiha Koma and Denen Dora members of the Hadar Formation (Beden 1985, Table 1) (Figs. 5–6). This mammoth is referred to by Beden (1985, 28) as more progressive than *M. subplanifrons* but more primitive than *M. africanavus*, known from the middle to late Pliocene of northern and central Africa (Coppens et al. 1978). The Hadar form reportedly is represented by a complete skeleton and ten or so skulls (Beden 1985, 28); one figured skull has the twisted tusks that characterize the genus (Johanson and Edey 1981, 96/97, Fig. 4). Beden (pers. com., 1976) suggests that undescribed molars (L246-1, -2) from the middle "Kalaloo beds" of the upper Sagantole Formation at Bodo (Fig. 4, Table 1) may be like the Hadar mammoth based on the overall morphology of these molars and their hypsodonty (108 on M_3). A partial molar (L240-1) from the Kalaloo beds in the eastern Matabaietu area may belong to this same form.

Although L210-1 is only a partial molar, it is nevertheless consistent with *M. subplanifrons*. The low crown, fused columns at the anterior end of the molar, and very broad, uniform, compressed and rectilinear loops are features comparable to the Langebaanweg M_3. Like L27-1a, the dimensions of L210-1 are smaller than the Langebaanweg M_3 as the lamellar frequency (LF = 4) is greater. The wrinkled enamel is a feature reportedly distinctive of early mammoths (Coppens et al. 1978, 357). Until more complete specimens of L210-1 – particularly skull and tusk material – are recovered, however, the identification of L210-1 is referred to tentatively as cf. *M. subplanifrons*.

Genus *ELEPHAS* Linnaeus 1758

The first fossil elephants known to have been recovered from eastern Africa are those of *Elephas* collected in 1902 in the lower Omo Valley by Emil Brumpt, a French naturalist (Beden 1985). We now know that this genus occurs throughout much of the Shungura Formation, and that *E. recki* is the dominant fossil elephant in the Omo Valley, as in the Middle Awash and the rest of the African Plio-Pleistocene. This species occurs throughout the upper Awash Group, from the middle Sagantole Formation to the upper Wehaietu Formation (Fig. 6).

Aguirre (1968) divided *Elephas* into two lineages: the genus *Palaeoloxodon* for the African-Eurasian group, and the genus *Elephas* for the Asian group. Following Maglio's (1973) interpretation that the two populations evolved from a common ancestor, and belong to a single genus, Beden (1983, 62) nevertheless felt the two groups have sufficient differences to distinguish them at the subgeneric level. Hence, Beden referred *E. recki*

to the subgenus *Palaeoloxodon* and the Asian *Elephas* to the subgenus of
the same name.

The earliest reported *Elephas* in Africa is *E. ekorensis*, described from
the Ekora beds, Kenya, by Maglio (1970a) (Fig. 3). This species is similar
to early *E. recki* but differs in cranium morphology and the distinctive
wedge shape of the M3. Metric features of molars of both species were
characterized by Maglio (1970b; 1973), in which he recognized four successive evolutionary "stages" of *E. recki* based on continuous morphological change of the molars throughout much of the Plio-Pleistocene. These
stages ranged from early forms with fewer plates, lower crowns, thicker
enamel, and less folding, to later forms with more plates, higher crowns,
thinner enamel, and greater folding. Using similar morphological criteria, Beden (1976, 1980a, 1981) later distinguished a fifth stage by dividing
E. recki Stage II into Stages IIA and IIB. Beden (1973, 1979a, 1980b, 1983,
1985) then assigned *E. recki* to five time-successive subspecies: *E. r.
brumpti*, *E. r. shungurensis*, *E. r. atavus*, *E. r. ileretensis*, and *E. r. recki*.
These taxa bear equivalence to the five stages in many respects but represent significant departures in terms of molar metric variation and the
reported age distributions of the subspecies. These differences are true
particularly for the later forms, based on greatly increased samples of
molars and refined dating of stratigraphic units from the Omo Valley and
East Turkana. Whether these subspecies will bear the scrutiny that
further collecting and study will bring remains to be seen, but for now
we retain Beden's classification.

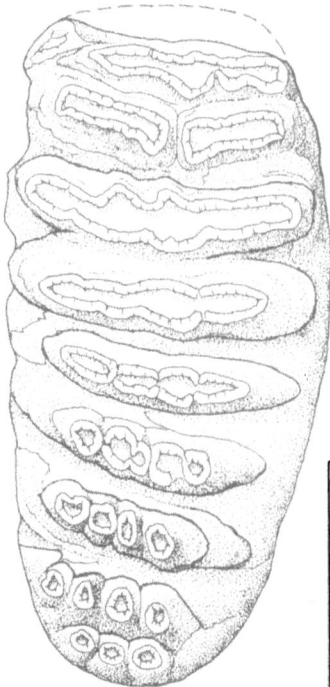

FIGURE 34. Right M₂ (L32-1),
Elephas recki brumpti,
Adu Dora, eastern Awash,
Sagantole Formation.
[SCALE = 5 CM]

ELEPHAS RECKI Dietrich 1915
ELEPHAS RECKI BRUMPTI Beden 1980b
(Figs. 34–36)

Specimens/Localities: L32-1, right M_2, Adu Dora East, L33-1, partial left M_3, L33-2, partial left M_3, eastern Bodo, L26-1, left M^3, eastern Wee-ee Dora, Aramis Member(?), Sagantole Formation (Figs. 2–6, Tables 1 and 4).

Description: L32-1 is a complete right M_2 with an M_1 root in a jaw fragment of a young individual (Fig. 34). The jaw is broken on either side of the M_1–M_2; the anterior ramus on the dorsal side is markedly downturned. The M_2 is 131 mm in length, with seven plates and anterior and posterior platelets (Table 4). The plates are moderately spaced (LF = 7) and low crowned. The plates are widest near their base and taper strongly apically. Valleys are U-shaped. The maximum width is 68 mm

Molar	Sp.	P	L	W	H	LF	ET	HI
				E. r. cf. *brumpti*				
M_2	32-1	7	131	68	--	6.5	2-3.3	--
M_3	33-1	+7+	140+	71	86	5	2-3.5	<121
M_3	33-2	+6+	105+	69	86	5	2-3.5	<125
M^3	26-1	11	192	70	50	6	2.5-3.5	71
				E. r. shungurensis				
dM_3	1-8	5	61	31	26	10	1-1.5	84
M_1	78-1	7	177	80	77+	4.5	1-1.5	96+
M_2	16-4	+5	112+	66	61+	5	1.5-2	92+
M_2	59-1	9	187	72	--	5	1-3	--
M_3	1-3	+8 1/2+	145+	70	≈87	6	1.5-3	≈124
M_3	23-1	12	192	≈70	≈80	6	2-3	114+
M_3	43-4	+9	167+	60	90	5	--	<150
M_3	67-1	+8 1/2	140+	73	72+	5.5	2-3.5	97+
M_3	68-1	+9	170+	75	≈90	6	2-3	≈120
M_3	71-2	13	245	68	63+	5	2-3	93+
?M_3	12-1	+3+	66+	78	105	6	--	135
?M_3	17-3	+4	70+	47+	74	≈6	2-3	<130
M^3	4-3	+6 1/2	142+	≈72	≈80	6.5	2-3.5	111
				E. recki recki				
M_2	31-1	10	227	85	--	5	1.5-3	--
?M	30-2	+4+	60+	73	135	≈7	--	185
M_3	108-1	+7	140+	70	120	6	1.5-3	171
M^3	194-1	+13	280+	81	162	5	1-2	200

TABLE 4. **Metric data for *Elephas recki* molars from the Middle Awash Valley.**

on the P2, tapering to 52 mm on the P7. Only the P1-4 are worn, revealing enamel loops that are curvilinear and slightly concave, with minimal folding and modest thickness (ET = 2–3.3). The P1 consists of two, widely separated hemi-loops. The P2 contains two, shallow, medial anterior folds separated by a broad, shallow indention. The remaining plates show decreasing wear with minimal medial expansion on the P3. Four apical digitations are present on the P5-7.

L33-1 (Fig. 35) and L33-2 are partial right and left M3 respectively from the same individual. The roots of both molars are missing. L33-1 consists of five full plates and two anterior partial plates; L33-2 consists of 5½ plates. L33-1 consists of the anterior part of the molar, probably the P2-7; L33-2 appears to be the P4-9. It is likely the number of plates on the complete molars did not exceed 11 or 12 in number. The length of L33-1 is 140 mm and 105 mm for L33-2; we estimate the maximum length of the complete molars to be 225–235 mm. The width of the anterior five plates of L33-1 varies from 67–71 mm, while the remaining plates, and those of L33-2, taper gradually posteriorly, reaching 50 mm at the posterior end of L33-2. The overall aspect of the teeth is elongated and narrow. Plates are moderately spaced (LF = 5); the worn plates stand out prominently as ridges between broad, U-shaped valleys. Only the anterior plates of L33-1 are worn, as is the anterior half-plate of L33-2.

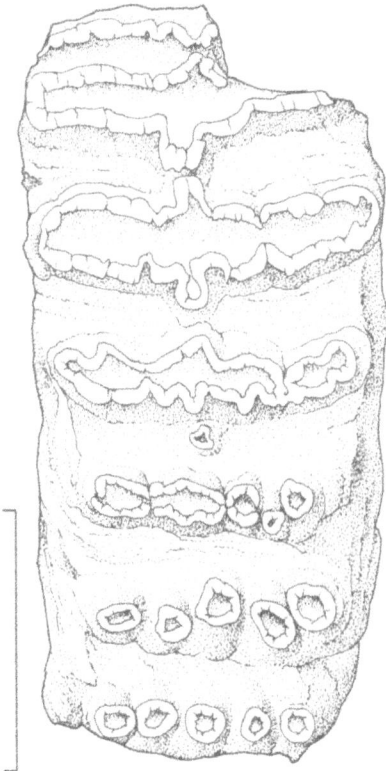

FIGURE 35. Right M3 (L33-1), *E. r. brumpti*, eastern Bodo, Sagantole Formation.

[SCALE = 5 CM]

The enamel thickness of these M$_3$ is modest (2–3.5). The height of both molars is 86 mm; the estimated hypsodonty is 121–125, less if the molars were posteriorly worn. The enamel loops are uneven, irregular, broadly folded, and asymmetrical with respect to the midlines of the molars. Opposing, prominent, irregular medial folds are present on the worn plates of L33-1, resulting from incorporation of medial pillars; the second full plate has a small, isolated posterior pillar. An isolated pillar is also present between two medial folds of the anterior half-plate of L33-2. Five to six apical digitations are present on the unworn plates of both molars.

L26-1 is a left M^3 with 11 plates and an anterior ridge (Fig. 36). The molar is well worn and nearly complete, except for a small anterior crown fragment and partial anterior root. The length is 192 mm and the height 46 mm. The hypsodonty is 66 and the plates are moderately spaced (LF = 6) (Table 4). The valleys are shallow (on a worn molar) and broadly U-shaped. The enamel is moderately thick (2.5–4 mm) with modest, even but tight folding. The enamel loops of all plates are curvilinear and

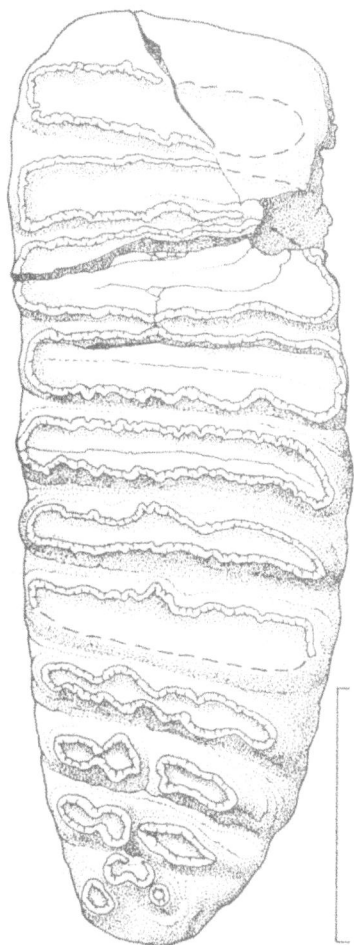

FIGURE 36. Left M^3 (L26-1),
E. r. brumpti,
Wee-ee, Sagantole Formation.
[SCALE = 5 CM]

slightly convex, particularly at the lingual lateral margin. P6-7 show some anterior medial expansion in the form of a simple fold just lingual to the midline. The enamel loop of the P8 is incompletely formed revealing five apical digitations. Plates 9–10 form half-loops consisting of paired apical digitations on each; two digitations are present on the heel. The loops of P1-4 are nearly touching, while the remaining plates are increasingly more distant. The widths of the P1-7 are fairly consistent (67–72 mm) with the maximum width occurring on P4-5; P8-11 taper gently.

Discussion: These molars are all consistent with early *Elephas*. Generally, this genus is characterized by molars with curvilinear enamel loops that are compressed laterally with localized, asymmetrical and commonly offset opposing or single medial folds. The convex-convex curvature of enamel loops is distinctive of upper molars of *Elephas* (e.g., Beden 1979a, Fig. 75, 1983, Fig. 3.18B, 3.24B), while concave-concave curvature of enamel is distinctive of lower molars (e.g., Beden 1983, Figs. 3.11C, 3.12A–B, 3.16B–C, 3.18A). In both cases, curvature is most pronounced at the lateral margins of molars. Medial expansion, observed as folds, is caused by longitudinal offset of the half plates, and also posterior pillars that are most prominent in the mid-height region of the molar plate. These pillars terminate just below the top of the plate and originate just above the base and, therefore, are absent at the very top and at the very base of the plate (Beden 1979a, Fig. 70). Posterior pillars are more prominent and attain a greater height on *lower* molars; anterior pillars are more prominent and higher on *upper* molars. Both anterior and posterior pillars are increasingly reduced in width in later forms of *Elephas* (e.g., compare L33-1 and Beden 1979a, Fig. 69B, 1983, Fig. 3.11C, 3.18, 3.22, 3.24). The more prominent pillars may be unattached to the plate, that is, free at their apex (e.g., L33-1; Beden 1983, Figs. 3.24 and 3.22).

Plate faces of *Elephas* are invariably uneven, irregular, and asymmetrical with respect to medial and lateral folding on either side of the midline of the plate. *Elephas* enamel loops seldom display the bilaterally symmetrical shape of *Loxodonta exoptata*. Medial folds on worn molars of *L. adaurora* are commonly offset laterally with respect to the mid-line of the plate, as in *Elephas*. The enamel loops of *L. adaurora* may show some curvature in a similar fashion as those of *Elephas*, but the overall shape of the enamel loop of worn molars of *L. adaurora*, at least *L. a. adaurora*, is more rectangular. Also, the lateral margins are more rounded while the plate faces are more rectilinear, and evenly and regularly folded.

L32-1 and 26-1 are characteristic of *Elephas* molars with light and heavy wear respectively, such that medial expansion is nearly absent in both cases, entirely so for unworn plates of L32-1 and heavily worn plates of L26-1. On the other hand, the moderately worn, anterior plates of L33-1 clearly reveal opposing, medial folds, with the greatest expansion present in the mid-height region of plates; the posterior medial pillars of the middle and anteriormost plates of L33-1 and -2 remain free at their apex.

The shape of the M_2 and M3 — ovoid for L32-1 and elongated for L26-1, L33-1, and L33-2 with the greatest widths occurring along the anterior 4–5 plates — is typical of *E. recki*, but differs from type molars of *E. ekorensis* from the Ekora beds, Kenya (Fig. 3), which are decidedly wedge-shaped (Maglio 1970a, Pl. VII-19, 1973, Pl. VIII-2). Beden (1979a, 354–355) has suggested that the marked, progressive, posterior narrowing of the Ekora molars represents an aberration of the true *E. ekorensis* population, and that typical molars of this species are more like those typical of *E. recki*. Beden notes cases where molars of *E. recki* narrow posteriorly more prominently than do other molars of *E. recki*; he suggests that such cases represent a rare morphological particularity rather than a true characteristic of the species. It may be, however, that Beden is partly referring to cases where modestly worn M3 (i.e., worn on the anterior 4–6 plates) of *E. recki* display a more elongated occlusal profile (e.g., Beden 1979a, Fig. 73B, 76A, 79, 1983, Fig. 3.22A), while *fully* worn molars display a more strongly tapered profile (e.g., Beden 1979a, Fig. 74A, 75A, 80A, 1983, Figs. 3.15B, 3.18). This is a result of the increased width of *E. recki* plates above their base (Beden 1979a, Fig. 91; Maglio 1973, Fig. 27F), such that the shape of a molar that is worn only anteriorly will display increased narrowing anteriorly, while the unworn posterior portion of the molar will be wider, giving the tooth a more elongated occlusal profile, such as L33-1 and L33-2. Otherwise, the Ekora holotype M^3, and the associated M^2 (Maglio 1973, Pl. VIII-2, identified as an M_2 in Maglio 1970a, 20), are unworn posteriorly, and if anything, these molars would be even more wedge-like with increased wear.

Even if Beden's suggestion is fully correct — and it probably is (see Roth 1989) — that *E. ekorensis* type molars are shaped more like those of *E. recki*, we feel that this needs to be demonstrated further. In this regard, molars Beden specifically refers to as being *E. ekorensis* — with an *E. recki* shape — come from the Usno Formation in the Omo Valley (Fig. 3). However, the Usno molars may be reasonably described as early *E. recki*, like or similar to *E. r. brumpti* from the lower Shungura Formation (Beden 1980b), while one of the few figured Usno molars, and the only complete M_2 (specimen W371), has an enamel figure similar to that of *L. exoptata* (Beden 1979a, Fig. 69A). We note that the metric characteristics of the Usno molars are within the range of variation of those of *E. r. brumpti* (Beden 1979a, Table 34; Beden 1980b, 1983, Table 3.13). Unfortunately, the Usno specimens are not associated with skull material that could be used to clearly distinguish *E. ekorensis* from *E. recki* (Maglio 1970a, Fig. 4A–B).

The metric characteristics of L32-1 and L26-1 (Table 4) compared to available data for *E. r. brumpti*, and the Usno *Elephas*, indicate a form significantly smaller in most respects than these elephants. The dimensions of L33-1 and L33-2, however, are like those reported of *E. r. brumpti*; the hypsodonty (121–125) is higher, but estimated from the unworn portions of the molars. In addition, the prominent, opposing medial folds of L33-1, combined with the coarsely folded, asymmetrical shape of the enamel loops, is unique to earliest *Elephas*.

Overall, it is apparent that early *Elephas* from the Middle Awash described above is a smaller form of *E. recki*. Since we know that L32-1 and L33-1 and L33-2 from eastern Bodo range between 3.8–4.1 m.y. (Table 1, Figs. 4–6), and perhaps L26-1 as well, then it is apparent that *E. recki* from the Middle Awash was contemporaneous with *Elephas* from the Ekora beds (Fig. 3), indicating that the two populations coexisted for a period, and had a common ancestor. In this regard, we note that Beden (1985, 27, Table 1) reports *E. ekorensis* present in the 30–40 m thick Denen Dora Member at Hadar along with *E. r. brumpti* (Johanson et al. 1978, 555). The age of the Denen Dora beds is uncertain, but falls within the time range of 2.88–3.35 m.y. (Fig. 6). By comparison, the Ekora beds, the type locality of *E. ekorensis*, are estimated to be between 3.75–4.0 m.y. (Fig. 3), or about the same age as *E. r. brumpti* from the Sagantole Formation (Fig. 6a). If these various identifications of *Elephas* are correct, then we can estimate that *E. ekorensis* and early *E. recki* coexisted in the Awash region for at least 0.5 m.y.

ELEPHAS RECKI SHUNGURENSIS Beden 1980b
(Figs. 37–38)

Specimens/Localities: L4-3, right M^3, L43-4, right M_3, L59-1, left M_2, L67-1, partial right M_3, L68-1, right M_3, L71-2, left M_3, L78-1, right M_1 Matabaietu D'ar; L1-3, partial right M_3, L1-8, dP_3, L12-1, partial lower molar (M_3?), L16-4, partial left M_2, L17-3, partial lower molar (M_3?), L23-1, left M_3, Wilti Dora, Matabaietu Formation (Figs. 2–6, Tables 1 and 4).

Description: L1-8 is a dP_3 with five plates, an anterior platelet, and no roots. It is worn the length of the tooth revealing irregular, wrinkled enamel loops that are rectangular-like, but expanded medially and along the lateral margins in concave fashion. Medial folds are simple and prominent on the anterior faces of plates and shallow and/or bifed on the posterior faces. The dP_3 tapers distinctively from a maximum posterior width of 31 mm on the P4 to 25 mm on the P1.

L78-1 is a complete, well-worn right M_1 in a jaw fragment (Fig. 37), with the partially crushed P1 of an M_2. Seven plates and an anterior platelet are present on the M_1. The P1 is rectangular-shaped while the remaining plates are increasingly compressed posteriorly. Enamel loops are concave-concave, irregular, wrinkled, and possess shallow anterior or posterior medial folds, or both, on the P1-5. The width of the molar is nearly constant on the P2-6 (75–80 mm), reaching maximum width on the P5.

L59-1 is a left M_2 in a jaw fragment (Fig. 38). The anterior half of the P2 is crushed. Plates 1-5 are worn into full concave loops that are moderately and irregularly folded and possess shallow medial accessories. Plates 6-9 are worn into partial loops containing 5-7 apical digitations. The anterior face of the P8 is missing, perhaps due to an abnormality at the time the plate was formed, in a manner like that described by Roth (1989). The M_2 is ovoid in shape: the maximum width (72 mm) occurs

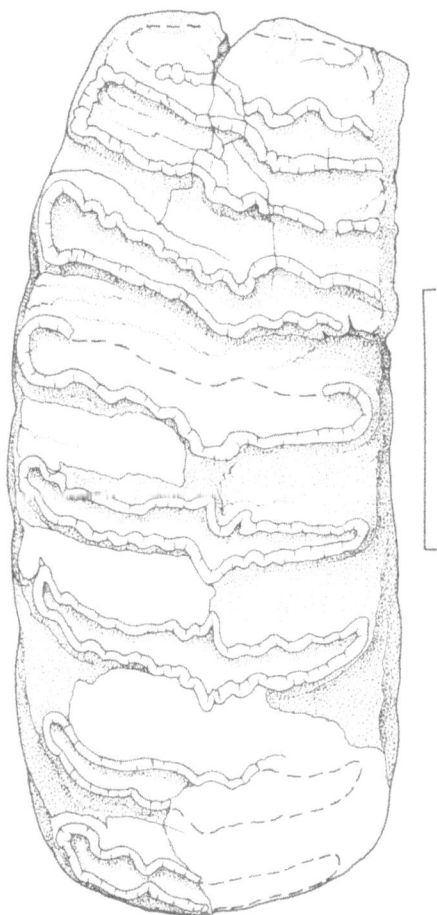

FIGURE 37. Right M_1 (L78-1),
E. r. shungurensis, Matabaietu,
Matabaietu Formation.

[SCALE = 5 CM]

at P6-7 with the width otherwise tapering gradually and modestly to both ends; the width of the last plate (P9) is 56 mm and 53 mm on the P1 (Table 4). L16-4 is a partial left M_2 with five posterior plates, a very small heel, and broken roots. This M_2 is more worn than L59-1 such that the anterior three plates (probably P5-7) are worn into full loops. The loops are concave, asymmetrical in shape, and moderately and irregularly folded. Opposing medial folds are present on the anterior two plates and posterior folds only on the third and fourth plates. L16-4 is similar to L59-1 in shape, but slightly smaller.

L71-2, 23-1, 1-3, 67-1, 43-4, and 68-1 are all M_3 in varying stages of completeness and wear. L71-2 is a left M_3 with 13 plates that is complete except for missing roots and a crown fragment on the buccal side. Only the P1-3 are worn into full loops. The overall shape of the molar is elongated and narrow, tapering posteriorly. Plates 5–10 are nearly uniform in width (66–68 mm); P11-13 taper prominently to 47 mm while P1-4 expand in width to 51 mm on the P1. L23-1 also appears to be a left M_3 although

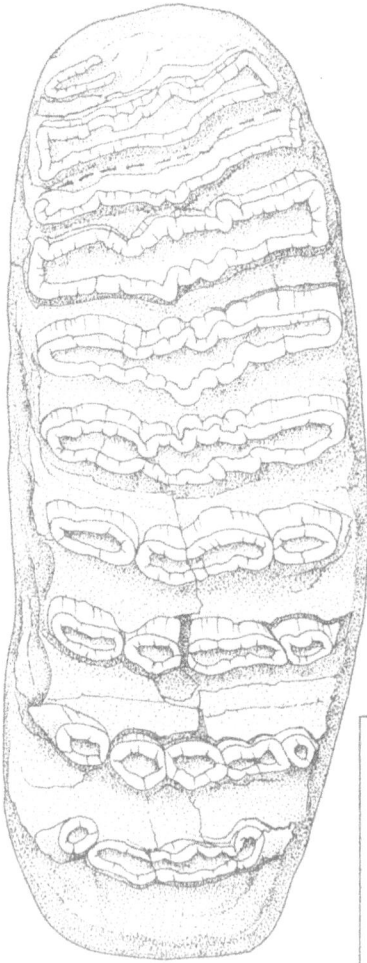

FIGURE 38. Left M₂ (L59-1),
E. r. cf. *shungurensis*, Matabaietu,
Matabaietu Formation.

[SCALE = 5 CM]

the entire buccal side of the molar is abraded. Twelve to 13 plates are present, as are the entire roots.

The remaining M₃ are all right molars. The anterior plates (2–9?) of L1-3 are present as are the posterior plates (P6–13?) of L67-1. The anterior three plates of both specimens are worn into full loops, which are modestly and irregularly folded like L71-2 and L23-1. L1-3 has prominent posterior medial folds, positioned lingual to the midline. The anterior two plates of L67-1 are modestly expanded. Both L1-3 and 67-1 taper posteriorly. L43-4 and 68-1 are partially erupted, elongate in shape, and show only anterior wear, almost none on L43-4 and modest wear on the anterior four plates of L68-1.

L12-1 is an unworn, partial lower molar fragment (M₃?) with three plates possessing six apical digitations on the anterior plate. The saggital section of the plates shows their expansion at mid-height. L17-3 consists of the posterior four plates of a lower molar (M₃?). The plates are unworn and possess five apical digitations on the anterior two plates, four on the next plate, and three on the last plate. The maximum width is 47 mm, which when complete probably did not exceed 57 mm for an M_3, less for an M_2. With a height of 74 mm, the maximum hypsodonty would be 130.

L4-3 is a right M^3 with 6½ posterior plates. The anterior two plates are worn into full enamel loops that are broadly folded. Four to six apical digitations are present on the remaining plates.

Discussion: These molars are typical *E. recki*. This is shown by their parallel, curvilinear, irregular enamel loops and medial features that are uneven with respect to the midline of plates. Enamel loops are distinctly asymmetrical, as illustrated in the anterior plates of the M_2, L59-1 and L16-4, and of the M_3, L71-2 and L1-3. The ovoid shape of the M_2 is typical of *E. recki*, as is the elongated, narrow shape of the M_3. The M_3 maintain a fairly constant width in the mid-region of the molar and taper strongest posteriorly, but not to the degree of the type molars of *E. ekorensis*.

The metric characteristics of these molars (Table 4) fall within the range of *E. r. shungurensis* or *E. r. atavus* from the middle Koobi Fora Formation (Beden 1983, Tables 3.18 and 3.23; Brown and Feibel 1986) (Fig. 3). The plate numbers of the dP_3 (P = 5), the M_2 (P = 9), and the M_3 (P = 13) (L1-8, L59-1, and L71-2 respectively), the overall size of the molars, and their hypsodonty favors closer comparison with *E. r. shungurensis*. Morphologically, the more moderate, even degree of enamel folding of the Matabaietu molars also favors this subspecies, as it is described from the upper Tulu Bor and lower Burgi members of the Koobi Fora Formation, and members C–E and lower Member F of the Shungura Formation (Beden 1979a, 1983; Brown and Feibel 1986) (Fig. 3). *Elephas r. shungurensis* is also reported from the Kada Hadar Member, Hadar (Beden 1985, Table 1) and from the upper Lomekwi, Lokalalei, and Kalochoro members of the Nachukui Formation at western Lake Turkana (Harris et al. 1988a, Tables 2 and 3, Fig. 2; Harris et al. 1988b) (Fig. 3). A form similar to *E. r. shungurensis* is present in the Geraru beds northeast of Hadar, and in areas north of Hadar at Houna [Hawoona], Ledi and Leadu (Taieb et al. 1972).

ELEPHAS RECKI RECKI Dietrich 1915
(Figs. 39–40)

Specimens/Localities: L108-1, partial left M_3, Dakanihyalo, lower Dakanihyalo Member; Matabaietu D'ar, L31-1, left M_2, L30-2, molar fragment, Wilti Dora, *Equus* beds; L194-1, left M_3, Meadura Dora, Meadura Member, lower Wehaietu Formation (Figs. 2–6, Tables 1 and 4).

Description: L108-1 is a partial left M_3, broken at either end, consisting of seven posterior plates of a molar that probably had twice that number when complete (Fig. 39). The maximum width (70 mm) is on the anterior

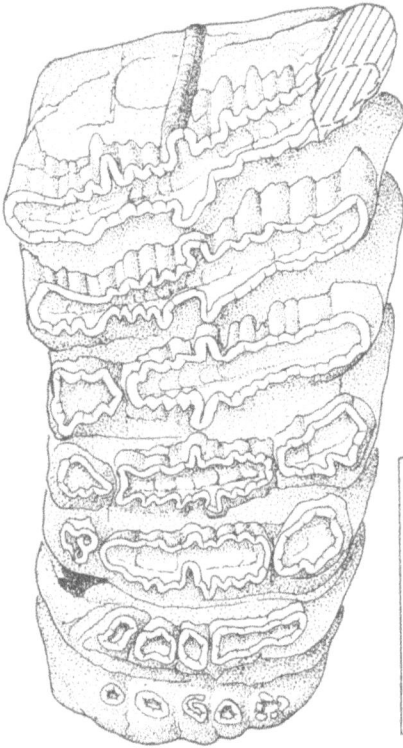

FIGURE 39. Left M_3 (L108-1),
E. r. recki, Dakanihyalo,
Dakanihyalo Member.
[SCALE = 5 CM]

two plates with the remaining plates tapering gently to 48 mm on the last plate. Plates are concave-concave, moderately spaced (LF = 6) and enamel is irregularly and finely folded. The M_3 is high crowned (H = 120) with a high hypsodonty (171). Only the first two plates form complete enamel loops; the remaining plates are increasingly divided posteriorly. Posterior medial folds are present on the first four plates, becoming reduced posteriorly with a reentrant fold on the fifth plate; smaller, medial folds are present anteriorly, also becoming reduced posteriorly.

L31-1 is a nearly complete left M_2 in a jaw fragment (Fig. 40); the anterior end of the molar is partially crushed. The remainder of the M_2 consists of the P2-9 and a posterior heel. The tooth is moderately worn revealing irregular, concave-concave, tightly folded enamel loops; only the P1-5 possess full loops. P5-6 have shallow opposing medial folds. The overall shape of the M_2 is distinctly ovoid with the maximum width (80 mm) occurring on the P4-6.

L30-2 consists of three unworn plates possessing up to six apical digitations. The plates are very high (132 mm) and hypsodont (183), even accounting for wear and a greater width on plates of the complete molar. The maximum width (73 mm), seen in saggital section, occurs one-third of the way above the base of the molar.

L194-1 is a left M^3 lacking only part of the anterior root. Thirteen plates are present, moderately worn the length of the molar. This M^3 is

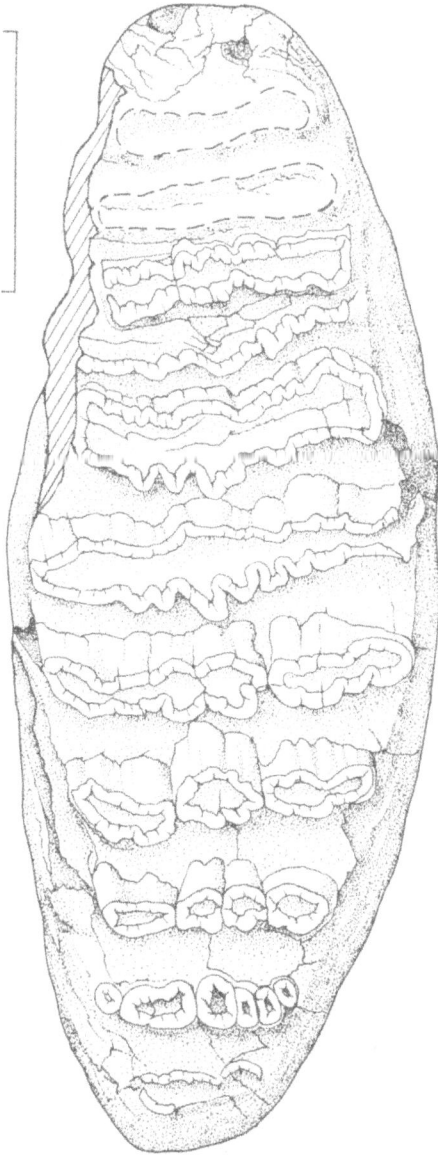

FIGURE 40.   Left M$_2$ (L31-1),
E. r. recki, Wilti Dora, *Equus* beds.
[SCALE = 5 CM]

very large, 280 mm in length, and reaches its maximum width (81 mm) at the P9-10, tapering to 70 mm at the P1 and P12. The enamel is very thin (1–2 mm) and finely wrinkled. The enamel loops are convex-convex and moderately spaced (LF = 5). Medial expansion is limited with simple, pointed, compressed anterior medial folds.

Discussion: These specimens from the lower Wehaietu Formation are all within the range of *E. r. recki* (Table 4), as described by Beden (1979a, Table 83; 1983, Table 3.32) from the lower Pleistocene of East Africa, notably from members K and L of the Shungura Formation, the Okote and

Chari members of the Koobi Fora Formation, Beds III–IV, Olduvai, and from the Olorgesailie Formation, Kenya (Fig. 3). Like L194-1—the largest elephant molar thus far reported from the Awash Valley—the other molars assigned to *E. r. recki* are all large in size, but with thin, finely folded enamel and reduced medial folds. Additional specimens recovered from younger sites in the Middle Awash also compare with *E. r. recki*, including fragmentary molars from the Meadura Member (L80-1) and the Bodo Member (L264-27, L283-1) (Table 1). L197-4a from Meadura consists of complete paired M^2 with maxilla and palate (partially covered with matrix). Fragmentary specimens from the Andalee Member (L191-149, L192-6) are consistent with *E. recki*, perhaps *E. r. recki*. Some of these specimens, especially the latter, may prove with full sample analysis to be equivalent to the late-surviving species, *E. iolensis* Pomel 1895, reported from isolated, middle to late Pleistocene localities in North Africa and South Africa (Maglio 1973, 37). This species is derived from *E. recki* as a terminal African form of *Elephas* (Maglio 1973, Fig. 15; Beden 1985, Fig. 2), and shows a continuation of the same trends that characterize the genus (Maglio 1973, 81).

DISCUSSION

The Earliest Elephantoids

The cladistic relationships of late Neogene proboscideans proposed by Kalb et al. (1992a) suggest that a longirostrine tetralophodont elephantoid is the sister taxon of brevirostrine tetralophodont "gomphotheres" on the one hand (the genus *Anancus*) and the Elephantidae on the other (Figs. 7 and 41). In this regard, the earliest elephantoid recovered from the Awash Group has been compared to *Tetralophodon longirostris*, a Tortonian-aged (6.7–10.4 m.y.) elephantoid known across Europe (Tobien 1978). The Awash fossil comes from the Chorora Formation on the Hararghe escarpment (Fig. 1) and consists of a single, nearly complete M₃ found by German geologist Markward Schönfeld in 1970. Although this specimen has not been fully described nor figured, reportedly it compares loosely with *T. longirostris*, and in certain features with *Stegotetrabelodon* (Sickenberg and Schönfeld 1975; Tiercelin et al. 1979, 257; Tassy, pers. com. 1982; Tassy 1986, 37). According to Tiercelin et al. (1979), the Chorora M₃ is large (L = 163+ mm, W = 86.5 mm), probably near 210 mm in length on the complete molar, and has six full lophids and a talonid. By comparison, *T. longirostris* from Europe has 5–5½ lophids on the M₃, while *Stegotetrabelodon* commonly has seven lophids on the M₃ (Tobien 1978; Coppens et al. 1978). The half-lophids of the Chorora M₃ are also aligned medially and possess one, sometimes two, posterior pretrite conules at the anterior end of the molar; very small secondary, posterior posttrite conules are also reportedly present anteriorly. The additional lophid(s) and accessory conules are derived features not present in *T. longirostris*.

Otherwise, *T. longirostris* (*sensu lato*) has been reported from a scattering of Tortonian-aged sites in North Africa, supporting the view of a European origin for the species (Coppens et al. 1978; Kalb et al. 1992b) (Figs. 41 and 42). More recently, a longirostrine tetralophodont elephantoid with a strongly downturned symphysis, provisionally referred to as *Tetralophodon* sp., has been described from the Namurungule Formation in the Samburu Hills, Kenya (Nakaya et al. 1984) (Fig. 3). These deposits are reportedly younger (≈8.5–9.5 m.y.) than the Chorora beds (10.5–10.7 m.y.) (Matsuda et al. 1984; Tiercelin et al. 1979). It is likely that the Samburu and Chorora specimens represent a progressive *Tetralophodon*-like lineage, the oldest representatives of which may have reinvaded Africa from Eurasia at the base of the Tortonian (~10.5 m.y.) (Fig. 41). This was a time of very significant lowered sea levels (Haq et al. 1988, Fig. 14), when faunal interchange was likely between Eurasia and Africa. In this

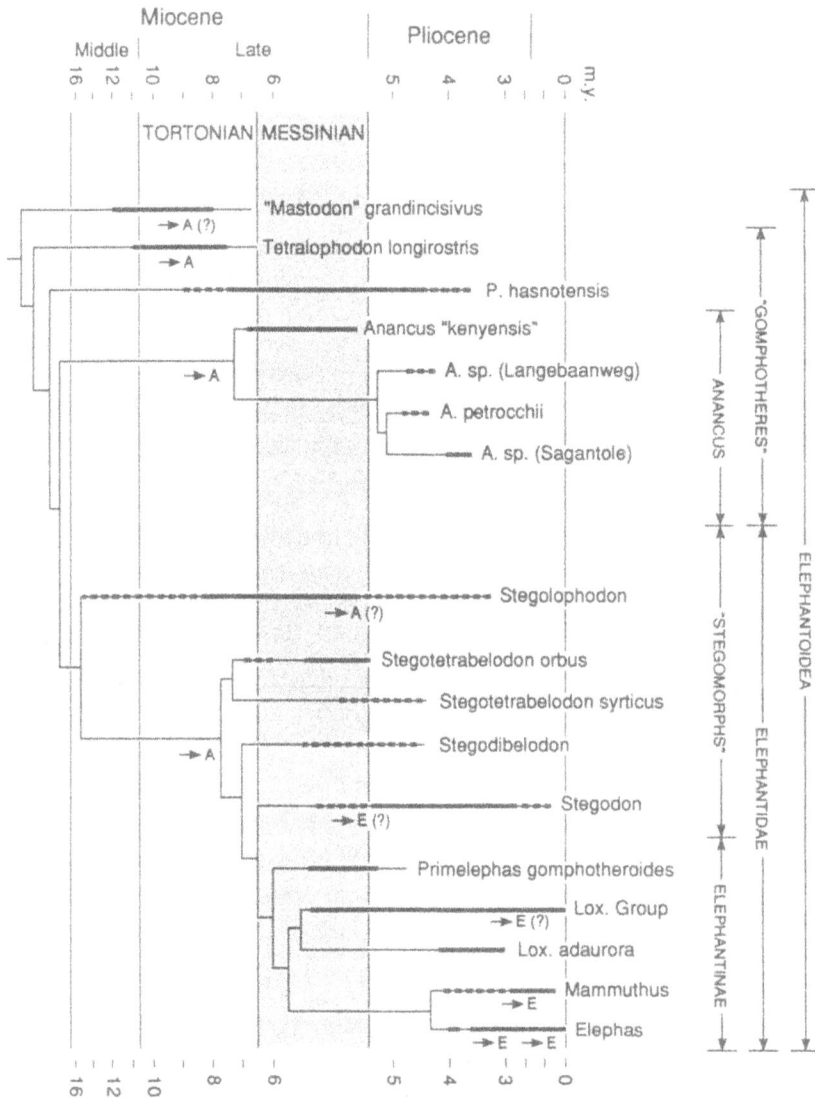

FIGURE 41. Phylogenetic relationships of late Neogene Proboscidea.

respect, *Hipparion primigenium* has also been recovered from the Chorora deposits, marking one of the earliest appearances of hipparionines in Africa (Jaeger and Hartenberger (1989, 410).

Tetralophodont *Anancus*

Kalb et al. (1992a) (Fig. 7) suggest that *A. "kenyensis,"* as it is known from Lukeino-A and the Middle Awash, is the sister taxon of a derived clade of tetralophodont (the Langebaanweg *Anancus*) and pentalophodont *Anancus* (*A. petrocchii* and the Sagantole *Anancus*). In terms of the

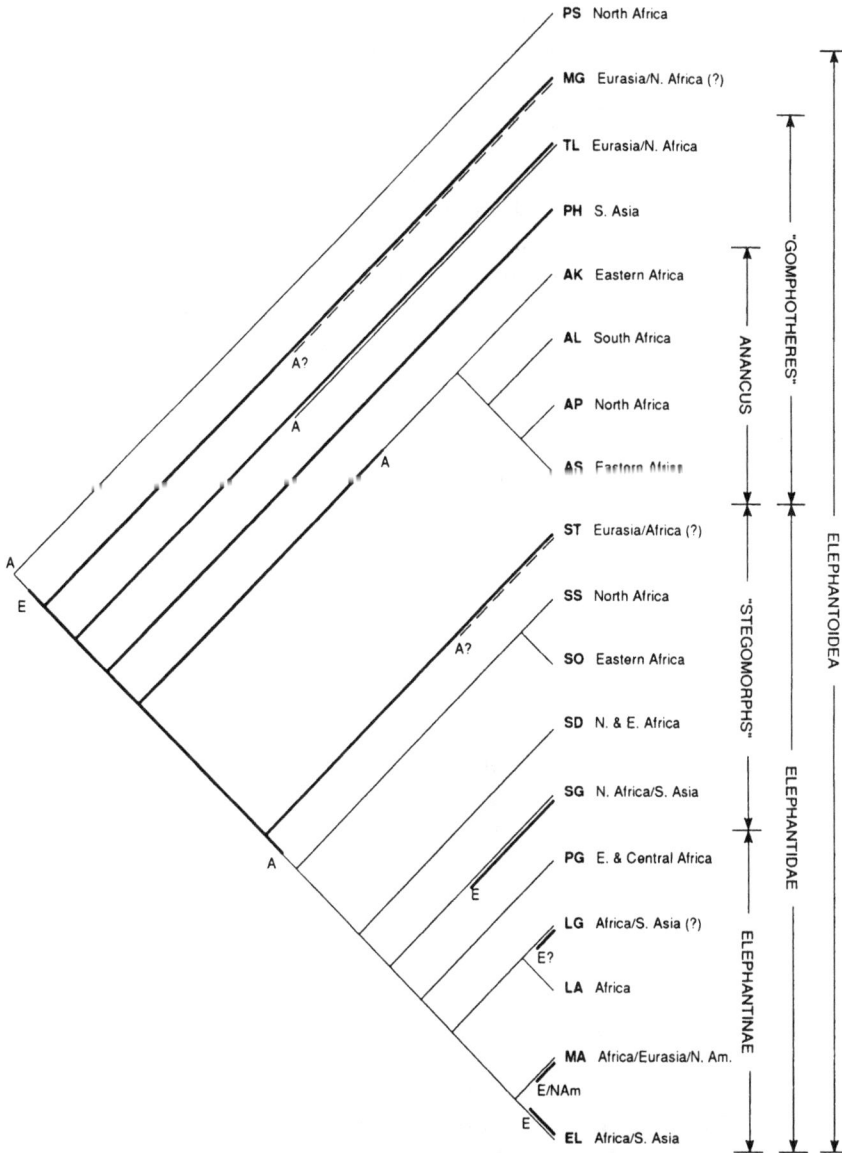

FIGURE 42. Geographical cladogram of late Neogene Proboscidea.

origin of *Anancus* in Africa, Tassy (1986, 103) has suggested that an
Anancus similar to the Eurasian *A. perimensis* may have immigrated to
Africa in the late Tortonian (~7.5–8.0 m.y.), a time that also corresponds
to a period of lowered sea levels (Haq et al. 1988, Fig. 14) and faunal interchange between Eurasia and Africa (e.g., Barry et al. 1985). Whether a
"proto-*perimensis*" is the common ancestor that gave rise to all other
Anancus is unknown. It is evident, however, that a conservative tetralophodont *Anancus*, *A. "kenyensis,"* like that from Lukeino-A and the Mid-

dle Awash, was present in sub-Saharan Africa near the base of the Messinian (6.7 m.y.) (Tassy 1986, Fig. 6). This date corresponds to a well-documented, renewed sea level regression, the onset of the Mediterranean "salinity crisis" (Haq et al. 1988, Fig. 14), a mass extinction of tetrapods (Benton 1989, 384), and renewed faunal interchange between Eurasia and Africa (Jaeger and Hartenberger 1989). At or near the end of the Messinian (5.2 m.y.), however, A. "kenyensis" became extinct and its sister taxon (the putative ancestor of more derived species of Anancus) gave rise to the Langebaanweg Anancus in South Africa, the Sagantole-type Anancus in eastern Africa, and A. petrocchii in North Africa (Fig. 42).

It may well be that global cooling and the lowering of sea level fostered the southward migration of Eurasian Anancus to Africa in the early Messinian, and the northward migration of African Anancus to Eurasia in the late Messinian (e.g., Bernor and Pavlakis 1987; Van Zinderen Bakker and Mercer 1986). These migrations would have been followed by the isolation of northern (European) and southern (African) Anancus populations accompanying the marine in-filling of the Mediterannean and Red Sea basins (Kalb and Jolly 1982; Girdler 1984; Stanley and Wezel 1985). For this reason, the European species, A. arvernensis, may have given rise to A. osiris of North Africa during the late Messinian, as proposed by Tassy (1986, Fig. 41). Otherwise, the in situ evolution of Anancus in Africa cannot be ruled out, particularly until more is known about the African fossil record between 7–9 m.y.

It is unfortunate that the species A. kenyensis was erected from such poorly preserved fossils—heavily worn or partial molars—which also come from sites, Kanam East and Kanam West, of uncertain age and stratigraphic context (MacInnes 1942, 82; Cooke and Coryndon 1970, 119; Tassy 1986; Pickford 1987) (Fig. 3). Nevertheless, the type M2 from Kanam East are clearly tetralophodont (Fig. 10B, K) and using this feature alone, we can readily distinguish this Anancus from more derived pentalophodont Anancus (Appendix, Table 1).

Of the fossils compared to A. kenyensis in the Middle Awash and Kenya, there is enough variation in features to distinguish provisionally early "conservative" forms from more "progressive" forms. The number of lophs varies from five on the M^3 of Anancus from Lukeino-A and the Kuseralee Member, to six on the M^3 from the lower Chemeron Formation; the lophid number varies from 5–6 on the M^3 from Lukeino-A to six on the M^3 from the Kuseralee Member (Fig. 10). We also note the absence of a talonid on the M_3 from the Asa Member (Fig. 11) and the Kuseralee Member (L216-6, L206-10) (Fig. 12), and its presence on an M_3 from the Chemeron Formation (Fig. 10Q). An increase in the number of accessory conules can also be seen when comparing the M3 from older to younger deposits, from Lukeino-A, the Asa, Kuseralee, and Haradaso members, Kanam East, and the Chemeron Formation (Fig. 3). The degree to which these trends are consistent in successive populations of A. "kenyensis" requires greater sample sizes to determine; however, at this stage it is enough to say that the Lukeino-A molars and those from

Kanam East and the Chemeron Formation represent the extremes of "early" and "late" *A. kenyensis*, while the Middle Awash form is intermediate between both.

Anancus from the Varswater Formation, "E" Quarry Langebaanweg, (Fig. 3) offers a clearer picture of a progressive tetralophodont *Anancus*, based on a representative number of excellently preserved molars (Fig. 10). These specimens have pronounced multiple, posterior posttrite conules on the M^2 and multiple enlarged, posterior posttrite conules and anterior pretrite conules on the M^3. These are clearly derived features absent in the Lukeino-A and Middle Awash *A.* "*kenyensis*," as described in detail by Kalb et al. (1992a). The Chemeron Formation M^3 (Fig. 10H) is more similar in basic respects to those from Langebaanweg; however, more conules that are distinctly enlarged are present on the Langebaanweg M^3. Cement is also present within the valleys of most, but not all, of the South African molars, which as previously mentioned probably relates to environmental and stratigraphic differences of the *Anancus* populations within the Varswater Formation.

An M_2 from Baard's Quarry, Langebaanweg—from deposits unconformable with the Varswater Formation at "E" Quarry—is also a large (L = 125 mm, W = 65 mm), very progressive tetralophodont, with a very enlarged talonid (Fig. 10L). This specimen is of uncertain age, but associated fauna suggests a somewhat younger Pliocene age than the *Anancus* from the Varswater beds (Hendey 1972, 1978; Gentry 1980, 327). The Baard's Quarry M_2 has posterior posttrite and pretrite conules the length of the molar, along with a second posterior pretrite conule behind the first and third lophids. In addition, the anterior lophids of this M_2 are distinctly aligned in a transverse manner.

All features combined, the Varswater molars may be regarded as a new, derived species of tetralophodont *Anancus* (Fig. 7); the Baard's Quarry M_2 may be a progressive form of this same species. Hence, while *A. kenyensis* was present in eastern Africa in the late Miocene, the more progressive tetralophodont from Langebaanweg was present in southern Africa in the early Pliocene (Fig. 42). In northern Africa, the species *A. osiris* was reportedly present from the early to late Pliocene (Tassy 1986, Fig. 41). This form is also a tetralophodont and may be loosely regarded as the northern African counterpart of the Langebaanweg *Anancus*. The molar structure of *A. osiris*, however, appears simpler (Tassy 1986, 100), although we suspect that specimens attributed to *A. osiris* (e.g., Arambourg 1970) may prove to be of more than one species.

Pentalophodont *Anancus*

Whereas *A. petrocchii* from Sahabi appears to be latest Miocene to early Pliocene, based on fauna (e.g., *Stegotetrabelodon*, *Stegodon*, *Amebelodon*) and regional stratigraphy (Boaz 1987, Gaziry 1987; deHeinzelin and El-Arnauti 1987), the pentalophodont *Anancus* from the upper Sagantole and Kanapoi beds is middle Pliocene in age, based on radiometric dates

($\approx 3.6 \leqslant 4.1$ m.y.) and fauna (e.g., Elephantinae) (Figs. 3 and 6a). The seven lophs of the Bodo M^3, the triple posterior posttrite conules of the Beearyada M^2, and the multiple conules of the Kanapoi M_2 are all derived features that characterize the Sagantole-type *Anancus* (Kalb et al. 1992a) (Fig. 10D, J, N; Appendix). The reported derived *Anancus* recovered from Kakesio, apparently from the lowermost Laetolil Beds (≈ 4.3 m.y.), may prove to be this same form (Harris, J. M. 1987; Hay 1987).

Elephantidae

The sister group of *Anancus*, the Elephantidae, is comprised of the paraphyletic "stegomorphs" and the Elephantinae (Fig. 7). The stegomorphs represent an informal, morphological "group" existing phylogenetically and morphologically between the gomphotheres and the Elephantinae (Appendix). *Stegolophodon* is the earliest known stegomorph and elephantid and it is the sister taxon of all remaining elephantids (Kalb et al. 1992a). It is a well-known Eurasian genus that may have made its way into Africa in the later Miocene, although the identification of the few specimens in Africa attributed to the genus (Petrocchi 1943, 1954; Hooijer 1963, 1970) is disputed (Maglio 1973, 17 and 53; Coppens et al. 1978, 359). A molar from Sahabi, Libya, in particular (Petrocchi 1954, Pl. 6) bears similarities to *Stegolophodon* (and to *Stegotetrabelodon*) and warrants reexamination.

The sister taxon of *Stegolophodon*, that is, the putative common ancestor of the remaining elephantids that coexisted with the earliest *Stegolophodon*, may have immigrated to Africa during the Tortonian (Fig. 41). Hence, it is likely that descendants of this proposed ancestor are of African origin, that is, *Stegotetrabelodon*, *Stegodibelodon*, *Stegodon*, and the elephants (Fig. 42). The only two known anterior mandibles attributed to *Stegolophodon* have shortened symphyses with vestigial tusk cavities (Tassy 1983; Sarwar 1977, Fig. 56; Tobien et al. 1988, Fig. 86), whereas the mandible and lower tusks of *Stegotetrabelodon* are fully longirostrine. While *Stegotetrabelodon syrticus* is known from reportedly early Pliocene deposits in North Africa, *Stegotetrabelon orbus* is known from late Miocene deposits in sub-Saharan Africa. Why *S. syrticus* may have survived longer in North Africa is unclear; however, this may relate to periodic isolation of North Africa during the Neogene, caused by climatic and environmental conditions analogous to those of today (e.g., Kalb and Jolly 1982). Otherwise, the only known locality of *S. syrticus*, Sahabi, may not be early Pliocene as reported (Boaz 1987), but may be late Miocene in age as was recently proposed by Geraads (1989). The absence of elephants at Sahabi and the presence of an amebebelodont (Gaziry 1987) lend weight to this argument.

Stegodibelodon schneideri can be described as an elephantid morphologically intermediate between the fully longirostrine *Stegotetrabelodon* and the fully brevirostrine *Stegodon*. There is no evidence of vestigial tusks in the Chad mandible (Coppens 1972), nor in the similar mandible from the Asa Member (Fig. 23), although vestigial tusks are apparent in the known mandibles assigned to *Stegolophodon* (Kalb et al. 1992a, Appendix I). The age of the Chad specimen is uncertain but its associated fauna (e.g., *Anancus osiris*, *Stegodon kaisensis*, *Primelephas korotorensis*) suggests an age, perhaps lower Pliocene, somewhat younger than the Asa Member (Coppens 1965, 1967, 1972; Kalb et al. 1982d).

Based on the cladistic relationships suggested by Kalb et al. (1992a), the genus *Stegodon* is the sister taxon of the Elephantinae. A predominantly Asian, Plio-Pleistocene genus, *Stegodon* has long been recognized as paralleling the African elephants in age and morphology (Osborn 1942). In the cladistic analysis of Kalb et al. (1992a), the paraphyletic association of *Stegodon* with earlier, more plesiomorphic *African* elephantids on the one hand, and later more derived *African* elephants on the other, suggests that *Stegodon* had an African origin (Figs. 41 and 42). In this respect, the limited known occurrences of *Stegodon* in Africa are all associated with one or more of the early elephantids, attesting to the early presence of the genus on the continent (e.g., Petrocchi 1943, 1954; Cooke and Coryndon 1970; Coppens 1965, 1967; MacInnes 1942; this volume). *Stegodon* from the Middle Awash (Figs. 24–25) may be among the earliest, if not the earliest, records of the genus in Africa. The apparent late Miocene to mid-Pliocene age of *Stegodon* in Africa, its limited distribution north of the Equator in Africa, and its abundance in Plio-Pleistocene deposits across Asia further suggest that *Stegodon* crossed from Africa into the Middle East and Asia in the early or middle Messinian (Kalb et al. 1992b). Evidence suggests that once free of competition from the other early elephantids (except, for a period, *Stegolophodon*) populations of *Stegodon* flourished throughout southern Asia.

Elephantinae

Based on the limited number of specimens available for *Primelephas*, evidence suggests that this genus is the sister taxon of, and shares a common ancestor with, the remaining elephants (Fig. 7). Based on the derived features that *Primelephas* shares with *Mammuthus* and *Elephas*, however—concave-concave enamel loops on the lower molars and a single posterior (pretrite) column—and its dissimilarities with the loxodonts—twin posterior columns in *L. adaurora* and convex-concave enamel loops in the *Loxodonta* Group (Appendix)—Kalb et al. (1992a) propose that *Primelephas* may form a clade with *Mammuthus* and *Elephas*. If the recovery of new fossil material from the Middle Awash and elsewhere shows this to be the case, the combined loxodonts would be the sister group ("Loxodontinae") of a *Primelephas*/*Mammuthus*/*Elephas* clade ("Elephantinae").

In regard to the above, we note that *Primelephas* and "cf. *Loxodonta*" (the basal member of the *Loxodonta* Group) are found contemporaneously in late Miocene deposits (5.5–6.0 m.y.) from Lukeino-A (Tassy 1986, Fig. 6). On the other hand, the earliest record of *L. adaurora* may be no older than the middle Pliocene deposits of Kanapoi, Ekora, Lothagam (Unit-3)

(Maglio 1973), and the Sagantole Formation (Fig. 3). The specimen from Wee-ee (Fig. 28) may be the earliest known record (3.8 ≤ 4.1 m.y.) of *L. adaurora* (Fig. 6a). Likewise, the specimens from Wee-ee which we ascribe to *M. subplanifrons* (Fig. 32) may be the earliest known mammoth (≤4.1 m.y.) (Fig. 6a), unless the individual from Langebaanweg proves to be older (Maglio and Hendey 1970) (Fig. 3). In this respect, we have noted that the South African molars are somewhat more derived than the Wee-ee molars. Coppens et al. (1978) identify molars from Kanam East as *M. subplanifrons*; however, we remain uncertain of this identification (we suspect this early elephant may be like the Lukeino-A loxodont) (MacInnes 1942, Pl. VII, Figs. 8–10). Finally, *E. r. brumpti* from the Middle Awash (Figs. 34–36) may be the earliest known record of *E. recki* (Fig. 6a), and of a similar age to *E. ekorensis* from Ekora, Kenya (Maglio 1973). We would expect these two species to be contemporaneous if they share a common ancestor (or vice versa).

Future Studies

Overall, it is clear that the fossil record of the early elephants in Africa is being pushed back further and further. Judging from how highly evolved are the molars of the Elephantinae (as we presently define the subfamily) compared with those of *Stegotetrabelodon* and the most progressive known African "gomphotheres" (derived *Anancus*), it is clear that significant morphological gaps still remain in the fossil record of the elephants, particularly in the 6–8 m.y. time range. We see, however, an emerging picture of what the earliest elephants must have looked like when we examine closely the few "early" elephants available to us; for example, the lower molars of *P. gomphotheroides* from Lothagam-1 (Maglio and Ricca 1977, Pl. 2, Fig. 3—see Kalb et al. 1992a, Appendix I), "cf. *Loxodonta*" from Lukeino-A (Tassy 1986, Pl. XIV-6), and *L. adaurora* from Wee-ee (Fig. 28). These molars have prominent posterior columns extending to their posterior end; on the unworn molars these columns are completely isolated. As remnant conules, the columns reflect trefoil patterns when combined with the half-loop ("half-lophid") configuration of unworn plates when median sulci are present.

An early *Elephas* from below the Tulu Bor Tuff (3.35 m.y.) at Koobi Fora (Brown 1982) identified by Beden (1983, Fig. 3.11-C) as *E. r. brumpti* reflects a similar condition. This particular *Elephas*, however, has *twin* posterior columns posterior to the P2-4, compared to the specimen from Bodo that we have identified as *E. r. brumpti* (Fig. 35), which has distinct, *single* posterior columns extending to the mid-molar. Otherwise, both the Koobi Fora and Bodo *Elephas* display the asymmetrical, irregular enamel loop pattern that characterizes the genus. The distinctions in posterior column development, however, reflect more plesiomorphic and varied forms and will eventually help us make more taxonomic distinctions based on dentitions between one form of early *Elephas* and another. At the same time, such differences in column placement will, we hope, allow us to distinguish more confidently isolated molars of early forms of this genus from those of its very poorly understood sister taxon, *Mammuthus*. Perhaps a thorough study of the Hadar-type mammoth reported by Beden (1985) – with the characteristic twisted tusks – and its putative ancestors in the Middle Awash (the Wee-ee type elephant) (Fig. 32) will shed new light, *any* light, on differences in molar development of *Elephas* and *Mammuthus*.

Hence, as more elephant fossils are recovered from the 4.0–7.0 m.y. time range it is likely they will more and more approach the "simplicity" and plesiomorphy of, say, *Stegotetrabelodon* molars, and their own particular ancestry. As these elephantids collectively approach their common point of ancestry, their morphologies will increasingly show convergent characters. Overall, the early elephantoid fossils from the Middle Awash uniquely reflect the transition from early elephantid to elephantine dentition.

The eventual recovery and study of the numerous elephantoid individuals we left uncollected in deposits of the Sagantole and Adu-Asa formations will certainly elucidate this picture. We point out that these fossils do not include simply isolated molars. For example, at the time the RVRME ceased fieldwork in the Middle Awash in 1978, we had mapped but not collected: three skulls of *Anancus* (at Kuseralee Dora, Beearyada, and eastern Bodo); a bone bed containing fossils of several *Stegotetrabelodon* individuals, possibly concentrated in a flood deposit ("the first '*Stegotetrabelodon*' family"?) (Saitune Dora); additional skeletal material of cf. *Stegodibelodon*, including a completely articulated foot (Adu Dora North); two localities containing additional fossils assigned to *Stegodon* (Saitune Dora and Adu Dora South); scatterings of *Primelephas* fossils (the Kuseralee Member); a partial skull of *L. exoptata* (Matabaietu); a skeleton of *M. subplanifrons* eroding from a crystalline tuff layer (the Moiti?) (Wee-ee); and probably a dozen skulls of *Elephas* (Gemeda, Wilti Dora, Matabaietu) (Fig. 3). Then at Hadar and immediately north and south of Hadar are scores of skulls of *Elephas*, *Mammuthus*, and *Loxodonta*. We can account for at least a half dozen localities in the Wehaietu Formation where elephant fossils (including possibly *L. africana* – L195-1) are found in association with Acheulian stone tools, although most of these specimens are fragmentary. One concentration of stone tools at Meadura also contains the partial remains of a very young elephant. Lastly, there are important elephantoid specimens recovered from different stratigraphic levels in the Middle Awash that are within the RVRME collection in the Ethiopian National Museum, which have not been available for this study, that will fill in more gaps in the fossil record.

"Specimens" of the modern African elephant, *L. africana*, can be seen occasionally today as bracelets on the arms of Afar nomads, that probably have been passed down from generation to generation. Interviews with older Afar men in the mid-1970s indicate that the last elephants in the Middle Awash Valley were probably killed off in the late 1920s or 1930s.

The word for elephant in the Afar language is "dakani." The name Dakanihyalo meaning "elephant ridge" is given by the Afar to an uplifted area on the southernmost flank of the Hatowie Graben (Kalb et al. 1982c, Fig. 3) (Fig. 3). The ridge overlooks a broad grassy plain and adjacent swamp that stretches along the Awash River for 20 or more kilometers depending on the rainy season. A multitude of wildlife inhabits this area and there is little doubt that multitudes of "dakani" remains lie at the bottom of this swamp.

Dakanihyalo is also an Acheulian tool site that has yielded the remains of *E. r. recki* (L108-1). Whether this is one of hundreds of butchery sites that surely exist throughout the Acheulian-tool bearing Wehaietu Formation is unclear; however, it does not require much imagination to speculate that elephants have been hunted by humans in the Middle Awash for tens of thousands, even hundreds of thousands of years, and longer. In great tomes, the archeologists will spell this out for us in the years to come.

In 1975, we were told by a very old Afar man—wearing an ivory bracelet—about seeing large white *dakani* bones along the banks of the Kesem River near its confluence with the Awash River. This area lies northwest of Awash Station (Fig. 1) in the extreme southwestern Afar Depression. It is also a well-vegetated, wet lowland, parts of which are cultivated today by a nearby plantation. The Afar explained that he had seen the bones there as a boy after his father had killed the elephant. One of us (JK) spent two days with the old man unsuccessfully looking for these bones—it must have been one of the last elephant "kill sites" in the Awash Valley. What would DNA fingerprinting and isotope analyses of the ivory bracelets tell us about the recent origins of the Awash elephants? And what would oral histories from the Afar people tell us about the fading memory of these magnificent but dwindling beasts?

CONCLUDING REMARKS

The one-kilometer thick Awash Group contains the most complete single record of late Miocene-Pleistocene elephantoids known in Africa. Represented are no fewer than 16 taxa, including two species of *Anancus* and the most complete series of fossil elephantids reported to date from one stratigraphic sequence in the Old World.*

Longirostrine-like and brevirostrine "gomphotheres" (the Chorora elephantoid and *Anancus*) are represented in the lower third of the Awash Group, while elephantids are present throughout all post-Chorora formations. Of the *Anancus*, two species are described, a tetralophodont comparable to *A. kenyensis* and a pentalophodont referred to as the Sagantole-type *Anancus*. *A. kenyensis* occurs throughout the Adu-Asa Formation, is particularly abundant in the Kuseralee Member, and is present in the lowermost Sagantole beds. This Middle Awash *Anancus* is clearly a conservative form. It is, however, apparently more progressive than the *"kenyensis-*morph" from Lukeino-A described by Tassy (1986), but perhaps—we suggest based on poorly preserved molars from Kanam East—not as progressive as the type specimens for the species. Certainly, the *A. "kenyensis"* from the Middle Awash and East Africa represent an altogether more conservative group of fossils than the advanced and previously undescribed tetralophodont *Anancus* from Langebaanweg. The additional, distinct conules on the upper molars of the South African *Anancus* are unique to this form, as the added conules and loph(id)s on molars of the pentalophodont *Anancus* from the Sagantole Formation and Kanapoi are distinct to this form. Study of the *Anancus* from Kakesio, Tanzania (Harris 1987, 525), may show it to be like the Sagantole-type *Anancus*. It is also apparent that near the time when the progressive Langebaanweg *Anancus* was a late-surviving tetralophodont living in southern Africa in the early Pliocene, the Sagantole-type *Anancus* was a late-surviving pentalophodont in eastern Africa (Figs. 41 and 42). Respectively, both forms may be loosely regarded as the sub-Saharan counterparts of *A. osiris* and *A. petrocchii* from northern Africa (Tassy 1986).

Following recovery of a more complete sample of the Middle Awash pentalophodont, the Sagantole *Anancus* can be more carefully compared

---

* Eighteen proboscideans have been identified to date from the Awash Group. These include: those described in this report; the "indeterminate gomphothere" from the lower Adu-Asa Formation (see footnote on p. 7); a progressive *Tetralophodon*-like elephantoid from the Chorora Formation (Tiercelin et al. 1979; see Discussion, this volume); *E. ekorensis* and a reported new species of *Mammuthus*, both from the Hadar Formation (Beden 1985); and apparently two species of deinotheres (Kalb et al. 1982d, 248).

to *A. petrocchii*, as further study of the progressive South African tetralophodont and *A. osiris* will allow closer comparison of these two forms.
Although Tassy (1986) has greatly added to our understanding of *A. osiris*
and *A. petrocchii*, only first-hand comparison of the fossils assigned to
these forms with those from sub-Saharan Africa will fully clarify their
morphological differences and phylogenetic relationships.

Accompanying the cladistic model suggested by Kalb et al. (1992a), we
have seen how the presence of prominent lower incisors alone distinguishes *Stegotetrabelodon* from all other elephantids, and how the elongated yet tusk-less mandibular symphysis of *Stegodibelodon* distinguishes
this genus from its fully brevirostrine sister group (Appendix) (Fig. 41).
Also, we have described how convex-convex shaped enamel loops of
lower molars of *Stegotetrabelodon* and *Stegodibelodon* are plesiomorphic features present in these two genera, and how the concave-concave enamel
loops in lower molars are derived features present in all elephants except
the *Loxodonta* Group, which has convex-concave shaped enamel loops on
well worn lower molars. Given the morphological similarities between
the genus *Stegodon* and the elephants, it is evident that both groups
adapted similarly to climatic and dietary changes in the late Neogene.
However, given the abundance of elephantids in Africa in the latest
Miocene (the late Messinian), we can suggest that *Stegodon* was simply
no match for the diverse elephantid, particularly elephant, populations
that were clearly widespread across Africa by that time.

The genus *Primelephas* may well be the "first elephant" as proposed
by Maglio (1973); however, based on its derived features shared with
Mammuthus and *Elephas*, Kalb et al. (1992a) have suggested that these
three genera may form a clade distinct from the loxodonts. We have also
suggested that "cf. *Loxodonta*" from Lukeino-A forms a clade with *L. exoptata*, *L. atlantica*, and *L. africana*, and explained why we feel this clade is
separate from *L. adaurora*. In addition, we have suggested that *E. ekorensis*
and early *E. recki* were contemporaneous in the early Pliocene, and
reasonably shared a common ancestor. And, we have added to the evidence (also present at Hadar) showing that early mammoths existed in
northeastern Africa, well north of the equator in the early to middle Pliocene, near the time that a somewhat more derived mammoth was
present in southernmost Africa (Langebaanweg).

Finally, although the Middle Awash elephantoids have filled in some
gaps in the fossil record of proboscideans, it is clear that major gaps
remain. In this regard, we have given a preview of what to expect in
molar morphology by way of remnant trefoil and remnant conule features. It is understood that continued collecting of fossils in the Middle
Awash Valley will significantly add to this picture.

By way of conclusion, E. Aguirre (1969, 1366) noted that elephants
"stand as a witness of prehistory." With the numerous hominid fossils
and many tens of thousands of stone tools documented in the upper
Awash Group, nowhere have fossil elephantoids and early hominids
been found to be so mutually abundant in a single area. Elephants were

as much a part of our prehistory and evolution, as we were of their evolution. It is interesting to ponder the words of G. G. Simpson (1945, 243) when he noted that "bewildering numbers" of proboscideans "had a much greater role in faunal history than one would dream from [the] impoverished representation" of the order today.

REFERENCES

Aguirre, E. 1968. Revisión sistematíca de los *Elephantidae* por su morfología y morfometría dentaria. *Estud. Geol.* (Madrid) 34: 107–116.

———. 1969. Evolutionary history of the elephant. *Science* 164: 1366–1376.

Andrews, C. W. 1904a. On the evolution of Proboscidea. *Trans. Roy. Soc. London* 196B: 99–118.

———. 1904b. Further notes on the mammals of the Eocene of Egypt. *Geol. Mag.,* n.s. 1: 109–115.

Arambourg, C. 1970. Les vertébres du Pléistocène de l'Afrique du Nord. *Archives Mus. nat. Hist. Nat., Paris,* ser. 10, 7: 1–126.

———. 1948. Les mammifères pléistocènes d'Afrique. *Bull. Soc. Géol. Fr.* 17(5): 301–310.

Aronson, J. L., T. J. Schmitt, R. C. Walter, M. Taieb, J.-J. Tiercelin, D.C. Johanson, C. W. Naeser, and A. Nairn. 1977. New geochronologic and palaeomagnetic data for the hominid-bearing Hadar Formation of Ethiopia. *Nature* 267: 323–327.

Asfaw, B. 1987. The Belohdelie frontal: new evidence of early hominid cranial morphology from the Afar of Ethiopia. *Jour. Human Evolution* 16: 611–624.

Barry, J., N. M. Johnson, S. M. Raza, and L. L. Jacobs. 1985. Neogene mammalian faunal change in southern Asia: Correlations with climatic, tectonic, and eustatic events. *Geology* 13: 637–640.

Beden, M. 1973. À propos des proboscidiens Plio-Quaternaires des gisements de l'Omo (Ethiopia). *Centre National de la Recherche Scientifique, Colloque International* 218: 693–705.

———. 1976. Proboscideans from Omo Group formations. In *Earliest Man and Environments in the Lake Rudolf Basin,* eds. Y. Coppens, F. C. Howell, G. L. Isaac, and R. Leakey, 193–208. Chicago: Univ. of Chicago Press.

———. 1979a. Les éléphants (*Loxodonta* et *Elephas*) d'Afrique Orientale: Systématique, phylogénie, intérêt biochronologique. Ph.D. diss., l'Université de Poitiers (France).

———. 1979b. Données récentes sur l'évolution des proboscidiens pendant le Plio-Pléistocène en Afrique Orientale. *Bull. Soc. géol. France* 21: 271–276.

———. 1980a. Repartition stratigraphique des éléphants Plio-Pléistocène en Afrique Orientale. 8ᵉ Reunion Annuelle Sciences de la Terre, Marseille. *Soc. géol. France,* 32.

———. 1980b. *Elephas recki* Dietrich, 1915 (Proboscidea, Elephantidae): Évolution au cours de Plio-Pléistocène en Afrique Orientale. *Geobios* 13: 891–901.

———. 1981. Données récentes sur l'évolution des proboscidiens pendant le Plio-Pléistocène en Afrique Orientale. In *Proceedings of the 8th Panafrican Congress of Prehistory and Quaternary Studies,* eds. R. Leakey and B. A. Ogot, 72–76. Nairobi: Intern. Louis Leakey Memorial Inst. for African Prehistory.

———. 1983. Family Elephantidae. In Vol. 2, *Koobi Fora Research Project,* ed. J. M. Harris, 40–129. Oxford: Clarendon Press.

———. 1985. Les proboscidiens des grands gisements à hominidés Plio-Pléistocènes d'Afrique Orientale. In *L'Environnement des Hominidés au Plio-Pléistocène,* Colloque international, Foundation Singer-Polignac, 21–44. Paris: Masson.

————. 1987a. Fossil Elephantidae from Laetoli. In *Laetoli—A Pliocene Site in Northern Tanzania*, eds. M. D. Leakey and J. M. Harris, 259–300. Oxford: Clarendon Press.

————. 1987b. *Les Éléphantides (Mammalia, Proboscidea): Les faunes Plio-Pléistocène de la basse vallée de l'Omo (Éthiopie)*, Cahiers de Paléontologie, Travaux de Paléontologie Est-Africaine. Paris: Éditions Centre National de la Recherche Scientifique.

Behrensmeyer, A. K. 1976. Lothagam Hill, Kanapoi, and Ekora: A general summary of stratigraphy and faunas. In *Earliest Man and Environment in the Lake Rudolf Basin*, eds. Y. Coppens, F. C. Howell, G. L. Isaac, and R. Leakey, 163–170. Chicago: Univ. of Chicago Press.

Benton, M. J. 1989. Mass extinctions among tetrapods and the quality of the fossil record. *Phil. Trans. Roy. Soc., London* B325: 369–386.

Bernor, R., and P. P. Pavlakis. 1987. Zoogeographic relationships of the Sahabi large mammal fauna (early Pliocene, Libya). In *Neogene Paleontology and Geology of Sahabi*, eds. N. T. Boaz, A. El-Arnauti, A. W. Gaziry, J. de Heinzelin, and D. D. Boaz, 349–383. New York: Alan R. Liss.

Boaz, N. T. 1987. Introduction. In *Neogene Paleontology and Geology of Sahabi*, eds. N. T. Boaz, A. El-Arnauti, A. W. Gaziry, J. de Heinzelin, and D. D. Boaz, xi–xv. New York: Alan R. Liss.

————. 1990. The Semliki Research Expedition: History of investigations, results, and background to interpretation. *Virginia Mus. Nat. Hist. Memoir* 1: 3–16.

Brown, F. H. 1982. Tulu Bor Tuff at Koobi Fora correlated with the Sidi Hakoma Tuff at Hadar. *Nature* 300: 631–635.

————. 1983. Correction of Tulu Bor Tuff at Koobi Fora correlated with the Sidi Hakoma Tuff at Hadar. *Nature* 306: 210.

Brown, F. H., and T. E. Cerling. 1982. Stratigraphical significance of the Tulu Bor Tuff of the Koobi Fora Formation. *Nature* 299: 212–215.

Brown, F. H., and C. S. Feibel. 1986. Revision of lithostratigraphic nomenclature in the Koobi Fora Region, Kenya. *Jour. Geol. Soc., London* 143: 297–310.

Brown, F. H., I. McDougal, T. Davies, and R. Maier. 1985. An integrated Plio-Pleistocene chronology for the Turkana basin. In *Ancestors: The Hard Evidence*, 82–90. New York: Alan R. Liss.

Brown, F. H., and R. T. Shuey. 1976. Magnetostratigraphy of the Shungura and Usno formations, lower Omo valley, Ethiopia. In *Earliest Man and Environments in the Lake Rudolf Basin*, 64–78. Chicago: Univ. of Chicago Press.

Burnet, G. T. 1830. Illustrations of the Quadrupeda, or Quadrupedas, being the arrangement of the true four-footed beasts indicated in outline. *Quar. Jour. Sci., London* (December 1829): 336–353.

Butzer, K. W., F. H. Brown, and D. L. Thurber. 1969. Horizontal sediments of the lower Omo valley: the Kibish Formation. *Quaternaria* 11: 15–30.

Bye, B. A., F. H. Brown, T. E. Cerling, and I. McDougal. 1987. Increased age estimate for the lower Palaeolithic hominid site at Olorgesailie, Kenya. *Nature* 329: 237–239.

Cabrera, A. 1929. Una revisión de los mastodontes Argentinos. *Rev. Mus. Las Plata* 32: 61–144.

Cerling, T. E., and F. H. Brown. 1982. Tuffaceous marker horizons in the Koobi Fora region and the lower Omo Valley. *Nature* 299: 216–221.

Chavaillon, J. 1979. Stratigraphie du site archéologique de Melka-Kunture' (Éthiopie). *Bull. Soc. géol. France* 21(3): 227–232.

Clark, J. D., B. Asfaw, G. Assefa, J. W. K. Harris, H. Kurashina, R. C. Walter, T. D. White, and M. A. J. Williams. 1984. Palaeoanthropological discoveries in the Middle Awash Valley, Ethiopia. *Nature* 307: 423–428.

Conroy, G. C., C. J. Jolly, D. Cramer, and J. E. Kalb. 1978. Newly discovered hominid skull from the Afar Depression, Ethiopia. *Nature* 276: 67–70.

Cooke, H. B. S. 1947. Variation in the molars of the living African elephant and a critical revision of the fossil Proboscidea of southern Africa. *Amer. Jour. Science* 245: 434–457, 492–517.

———. 1978. Faunal evidence for the biotic setting of early African hominids. In *Early Hominids of Africa*, 267–281. New York: St. Martin's Press.

———. 1986. Changing perspectives on the age of man (a geologist's personal view). Witwaterstrand University Press (South Africa), *Raymond Dart Lectures* (September 1983) 21: 1–46.

Cooke, H. B. S., and S. Coryndon. 1970. Fossil mammals from the Kaiso Formation and other related deposits in Uganda. In Vol. 2, *Fossil Vertebrates of Africa*, eds. L. S. B. Leakey and R. J. G. Savage, 107–224. London: Academic Press.

Coppens, Y. 1965. Les proboscidiens du Tchad, leur contribution à la chronologie du Quaternaire Africain. In *Actes du Ve Congrès Panafrican de Préhistoire et de l'étude de Quaternaire*, 331–387. Santa Cruz de Tenerife (Canarias): Museo Arqueólogico de Tenerife.

———. 1967. Les faunes de vertèbres Quaternaires du Chad. In *Background to Evolution in Africa*, eds. W. W. Bishop and J. D. Clark, 89–97. Chicago: Univ. of Chicago Press.

———. 1972. Un nouveau proboscidean de Pliocène du Tchad, *Stegodibelodon schneideri* nov. gen. nov. sp., et le phylum des Stegotetrabelodontinae. *C. R. Acad. Sci., Paris* 274: 2962–2965.

Coppens, Y., V. J. Maglio, C. T. Madden, and M. Beden. 1978. Proboscidea. In *Evolution of African Mammals*, eds. V. J. Maglio and H. B. S. Cooke, 336–367. Cambridge: Harvard Univ. Press.

Corvinus, G. 1976. Prehistoric exploration at Hadar, Ethiopia. *Nature* 261: 571–572.

Corvinus, G., and H. Roche. 1980. Prehistoric exploration at Hadar in the Afar (Ethiopia) in 1973, 1974 and 1976. In *Proceedings of the 8th Panafrican Congress of Prehistory and Quaternary Studies Nairobi, (September 1977)*, eds. R. Leakey and B. A. Ogot, 189–193. Nairobi: Intern. Louis Leakey Memorial Inst. for African Prehistory.

Cuvier, Frédéric, and E. Geoffroy Saint-Hilaire. 1825. *Histoire naturelle des mammifères*, III. Livr. LI, LII.

Dart, R. 1929. Mammoths and other fossil elephants of the Vaal and Limpopo watersheds. *S. Afr. Jour. Sci.* 26: 698–731.

Dietrich, W. O. 1915. *Elephas antiquus recki* n.f. aus dem Diluvium Deutsch-Ostafrikas. In *Oldoway Expedition*, ed. H. Reck, 80. Leipzig.

———. 1941. Die Säugetierpaläontologischen Ergebnisse der Kohl-Larsen'schen Expedition 1937–1939 im nördlichen Deutsch-Ostafrika. *Zentralbl. Min. Geol. Pal.* (Stuttgart) B: 217–223.

Drake, R., and G. H. Curtis. 1987. K-Ar geochronology of the Laetoli fossil localities. In *Laetoli—A Pliocene Site in Northern Tanzania*, eds. M. D. Leakey and J. M. Harris, 48–52. Oxford: Clarendon Press.

Falconer, H. 1857. On the species of mastodon and elephant occurring in the fossil state in Great Britain. Part I. Mastodon. *Quar. Jour. Geol. Soc., London* 13: 307–360.

Fitch, F. J., and J. A. Miller. 1976. Conventional Potassium-Argon and Argon-40/ Argon-39 dating of the volcanic rocks from East Rudolf. In *Earliest Man and Environments in the Lake Rudolf Basin*, eds. Y. Coppens, F. C. Howell, G. L. Isaac, and R. Leakey, 123–147. Chicago: Univ. of Chicago Press.

Gaziry, A. W. 1982. Proboscidea from the Sahabi Formation. *Garyounis Sci. Bull.* (Libya) 4: 101–108.

———. 1987. Remains of Proboscidea from the early Pliocene of Sahabi, Libya. In *Neogene Paleontology and Geology of Sahabi*, eds. N. T. Boaz, A. El-Arnauti, A. W. Gaziry, J. de Heinzelin, and D. D. Boaz, 183–203. New York: Alan R. Liss.

Gentry, A. W. 1980. Fossil Bovidae (Mammalia) from Langebaanweg, South Africa. *Ann. S. Afr. Mus.* 79: 213–337.

———. 1981. Notes on Bovidae (Mammalia) from the Hadar Formation, and from Amado and Geraru, Ethiopia. *Kirtlandia* 33: 1–30.

Geraads, D. 1985. La faune des gisements de Melka Kunturé (Éthiopie). In *L'Environnement des Hominides au Plio-Pléistocène*, Colloque international, Fondation Singer-Polignac, 165–174. Paris: Masson.

———. 1989. Vertèbres fossiles du Miocène supérieur du Djebel Krechem El Artsouma (Tunisie centrale). *Geobios* 22: 777–801.

Géze, R. 1985. Répartition paléoécologique et relations phylogénétiques des Hippopotamidae (Mammalia, Artiodactyla) du Néogène d'Afrique Orientale. *L'Environnement des Hominides au Plio-Pléistocène*, Colloque international, Fondation Singer-Polignac, 81–100. Paris: Masson.

Girard, C. 1852. On the classification of Mammalia. *Proc. Amer. Assoc. Adv. Sci., Annual Meeting*: 319–335.

Girdler, R. W. 1984. The evolution of the Gulf of Aden and Red Sea in space and time. In *Marine Science of the North-West Indian Ocean and Adjacent Waters*, ed. M. V. Angel, 747–762. Oxford: Pergamon Press.

Gortani, M., and A. Bianchi. 1938. Osservazioni geologiche e petrografiche sulla Dancalia meridionale e zone contermini. *Boll. Soc. Geol. Ital.* 57: 353–365.

———. 1941a. Note illustrative su la carta geologica degli altipiani Hararini e della Dancalia meridionale. *Mem. Accad. Sci. Isti. di Bologna* 8: 89–104.

———. 1941b. *Carta geologica degli altipiani Hararini e della Dancalia meridionale (scala 1:500,000)*. Roma: Reale Accad. Italia.

Gowlett, J. A. 1987. New dates for the Acheulian age. *Nature* 329: 200.

Gray, B. T. 1980. Environmental reconstruction of the Hadar Formation (Afar, Ethiopia). Ph.D. diss., Case Western Reserve University, Cleveland.

Gray, J. E. 1821. On the natural arrangement of vertebrate animals. *London Med. Repository* 15(88): 296–310.

Haileab, B., and F. H. Brown. (1992). Turkana Basin-Middle Awash Valley correlations and the age of the Sagantole and Hadar formations. *Jour. Human Evol.* 22: 453–468.

Hall, C. M., R. C. Walter, J. A. Westgate, and D. York. 1984. Geochronology, stratigraphy, and geochemistry of Cindery Tuff in Pliocene hominid-bearing sediments of the Middle Awash, Ethiopia. *Nature* 308: 26–31.

Hall, C. M., R. C. Walter, and D. York. 1985. Tuff above "Lucy" is over 3 MA old. *EOS* 66: 257.

Haq, B. U., J. Hardenbol, and P. R. Vail. 1988. Mesozoic and Cenozoic chronostratigraphy and cycles of sea-level change. In *Sea-level Changes: An Integrated Approach*, eds. C. K. Wilgus, B. S. Hastings, C. G. Kendall, H. W. Posamentier, C. A. Ross, and J. C. Van Wagoner, 71–108. Special Publication 42. Tulsa: Society of Economic Paleontologists and Mineralogists.

Harland, W. B., R. L. Armstrong, A. V. Cox, L. E. Craig, A. G. Smith, and D. G. Smith. 1990. *A Geologic Time Scale*. Cambridge: Cambridge Univ. Press.

Harris, J. M. 1987. Summary. In *Laetoli—A Pliocene Site in Northern Tanzania*, eds. M. D. Leakey and J. M. Harris, 524–532. Oxford: Clarendon Press.

Harris, J. M., F. H. Brown, M. G. Leakey, A. C. Walker, and R. Leakey. 1988a. Pliocene and Pleistocene hominid-bearing sites from west of Lake Turkana, Kenya. *Science* 239: 27–33.

Harris, J. M., F. H. Brown, and M. G. Leakey. 1988b. Stratigraphy and paleontology of Pliocene and Pleistocene localities west of Lake Turkana, Kenya. *Nat. Hist. Mus. Los Angeles County, Contributions in Science* 399: 1–128.

Harris, J. M., and T. D. White. 1979. Evolution of the Plio-Pleistocene African Suidae. *Trans. Amer. Phil. Soc.* 69(2): 1–128.

Harris, J. W. 1983. Cultural beginnings: Plio-Pleistocene archaeological occurrences from the Afar. Ethiopia. *Afr. Arch. Rev.* 1: 3–31.

Hay, O. P. 1922. Further observations on some extinct elephants. *Proc. Biol. Soc. Washington* 35: 97–102.

Hay, R. L. 1981. Paleoenvironments of the Laetolil Beds, northern Tanzania. In *Hominid Sites: Their Geologic Setting*, eds. G. Rapp Jr. and C. F. Vondra, 7–24. Boulder: Amer. Assoc. Advancement of Science.

———. 1987. Geology of the Laetoli area. In *Laetoli—A Pliocene Site in Northern Tanzania*, eds. M. D. Leakey and J. M. Harris, 23–47. Oxford: Clarendon Press.

de Heinzelin, J., ed. 1983. *The Omo Group—Archives of the International Omo Research Expedition*. Tervuren (Belgique): Mus. Roy. l'Afrique Centrale.

de Heinzelin, J., and A. El-Arnauti. 1987. The Sahabi Formation and related deposits. In *Neogene Paleontology and Geology of Sahabi*, eds. N. T. Boaz, A. El-Arnauti, A. W. Gaziry, J. de Heinzelin, and D. D. Boaz, 1–22. New York: Alan R. Liss.

Hendey, Q. B. 1970a. The age of the fossiliferous deposits at Langebaanweg, Cape Province. *Ann. S. Afr. Mus.* 56: 119–131.

———. 1970b. A review of the geology and palaeontology of the Plio-Pleistocene deposits at Langebaanweg, Cape Province. *Ann. S. Afr. Mus.* 56: 75–117.

———. 1972. Further observations on the age of the mammalian fauna from Langebaanweg, Cape Province. *Paleoecology of Africa* 6: 172–175.

———. 1978. The age of the fossils from Baard's Quarry, Langebaanweg, South Africa. *Ann. S. Afr. Mus.* 75(1): 1–24.

———. 1984. Southern African late Tertiary vertebrates. In *Southern African Prehistory and Paleoenvironments*, ed. R. G. Klein, 81–395. Rotterdam: A. A. Balkema.

Henning, W. 1966. *Phylogenetic Systematics*. Urbana: Univ. of Illinois.

Hill, A. 1985. Les variations de la faune du Miocène récent et du Pliocène d'Afrique de l'Est. *L'Anthropologie* 89: 275–279.

Hill, A., G. Curtis, and R. Drake. 1986. Sedimentary stratigraphy of the Tugen Hills, Baringo, Kenya. In *Sedimentation in the African Rifts*, eds. L. E. Frostick, R. W. Renaut, I. Reid, and J. J. Tiercelin, 285–295. Special Publication 25. London: Geological Society.

Hill, A., R. Drake, L. Tauxe, M. Monaghan, J. C. Barry, A. K. Behrensmeyer, G. Curtis, B. Jacobs, L. Jacobs, N. Johnson, and D. Pilbeam. 1985. Neogene palaeontology and geochronology of the Baringo basin, Kenya. *Jour. Human Evol.* 141: 759–773.

Hooijer, D. A. 1963. Miocene Mammalia of Congo. *Ann. Mus. Roy. Afr. Centrale, Sci. géol. Tervuren* 46: 1–77.

———. 1970. Miocene Mammalia of Congo, a correction. *Ann. Mus. Roy. Afr. Centrale, sci. géol. Tervuren* 67: 161–167.

Hopwood, A. T. 1935. Fossil Proboscidea from China. *Palaeont. Sinica*, ser. C, 9: 1–108.

——. 1939. The mammalian fossils. In *The Prehistory of Uganda Protectorate*, T. P. O'Brien, 308–316. Cambridge: Cambridge Press.

Howell, F. C. 1978. Hominidae. In *Evolution of African Mammals*, eds. V. J. Maglio and H. B. S. Cooke, 154–248. Cambridge: Harvard Univ. Press.

Isaac, G. L. 1977. *Olorgesailie*. Chicago: Univ. of Chicago Press.

——. 1978. The Olorgesailie Formation: Stratigraphy, tectonics, and the palaeo-geographic context of the Middle Pleistocene archaeological sites. In *Geological Background to Fossil Man*, ed. W. W. Bishop, 173–206. Edinburgh: Scottish Academic Press.

Jaeger, J.-J., and J.-J. Hartenberger. 1989. Diversification and extinction patterns among Neogene perimediterranean mammals. *Phil. Trans. Roy. Soc. London* B325: 401–420.

James, C., and G. Demissie. 1971. Geologic map of the southern Afar (1:250,000). Ethiopian Geological Survey, Addis Ababa.

Johanson, D. C., M. Taieb, B. T. Gray, and Y. Coppens. 1978. Geological framework of the Pliocene Hadar Formation (Afar Ethiopia) with notes on paleontology including hominids. In *Geological Background to Fossil Man*, ed. W. W. Bishop, 549–564. Edinburgh: Scottish Academic Press.

Johanson, D. C., M. Taieb, and Y. Coppens. 1982. Pliocene hominids from the Hadar Formation, Ethiopia (1973–1977): Stratigraphic, chronologic, and paleoenvironmental contexts, with notes on hominid morphology and systematics. *Amer. Jour. Phy. Anthro.* 57: 373–402.

Kalb, J. E., ed. 1976. Rift Valley Research Mission in Ethiopia. Annual Report, 1975–1976, Report to the Ethiopian Ministry of Culture (Addis Ababa) No. 8: 1–182.

——, ed. 1977. Rift Valley Research Mission in Ethiopia. Annual Report, 1976–1977. Report to the Ethiopian Ministry of Culture (Addis Ababa) No. 23: 1–432.

——. 1978. Mio-Pleistocene deposits in the Afar Depression, Ethiopia. *Sinet: Ethiopian Jour. Sci.* 1(2): 87–98.

——. (1993; in press). Refined stratigraphy of the hominid-bearing Awash Group, Middle Awash Valley, Ethiopia. *Newsl. Stratig.*

Kalb, J. E., D. J. Froehlich, and G. L. Bell. (1992a; in press). Phylogeny of African and Eurasian Elephantoidea of the late Neogene. In *The Proboscidea: Trends in Evolution and Paleoecology*, eds. J. Shoshani and P. Tassy. Oxford: University Press.

——. (1992b; in press). Paleobiogeography of late Neogene African and Eurasian Elephantoidea. In *The Proboscidea: Trends in Evolution and Paleoecology*, eds. J. Shoshani and P. Tassy. Oxford: University Press.

Kalb, J. E., M. Jaeger, C. J. Jolly, and B. Kana. 1982a. Preliminary geology, paleontology, and paleoecology of a Sangoan site in the Middle Awash Valley, Ethiopia. *Jour. Arch. Sci.* 9: 349–363.

Kalb, J. E., and C. J. Jolly. 1982. Late Miocene and early Pliocene formations in the Middle Awash Valley, Ethiopia, and their bearing on the zoogeography of Sahabi. *Garyounis Sci. Bull.* (Libya) 4: 123–132.

Kalb, J. E., C. J. Jolly, A. Mebrate, S. Tebedge, C. Smart, E. B. Oswald, D. Cramer, P. Whitehead, C. B. Wood, G. C. Conroy, T. Adefris, L. Sperling, and B. Kana. 1982b. Fossil mammals and artifacts from the Middle Awash Valley, Ethiopia. *Nature* 298: 17–25.

Kalb, J. E., C. J. Jolly, E. B. Oswald, and P. Whitehead. 1984. Early hominid habitation in Ethiopia. *Amer. Scientist* 72: 168–178.

Kalb, J. E., E. B. Oswald, A. Mebrate, S. Tebedge, and C. J. Jolly. 1982c. Stratigraphy of the Awash Group, Middle Awash Valley, Afar, Ethiopia. *Newsl. Stratig.* 11(31): 95–127.

Kalb, J. E., E. B. Oswald, A. Mebrate, S. Tebedge, C. Smart, E. B. Oswald, P. Whitehead, C. W. Wood, T. Adefris, and V. Rawn-Schatzinger. 1982d. Vertebrate faunas from the Awash Group, Middle Awash Valley, Afar, Ethiopia. *Jour. Vert. Paleont.* 2(2): 237–258.

Kalb, J. E., E. B. Oswald, S. Tebedge, A. Mebrate, E. Tola, and D. Peak. 1982e. Geology and stratigraphy of Neogene deposits, Middle Awash Valley, Afar, Ethiopia. *Nature* 298: 25–29.

Kalb, J. E., and D. Peak. 1975. Documentation of fossil sites along the lower Awash Valley in the Afar region. Report to the Ethiopian Antiquities Administration [Ethiopian Ministry of Culture and Sports Affairs] (Addis Ababa).

Kalb, J. E., C. Wood, C. Smart, E. Oswald, A. Mebrate, S. Tebedge, and P. Whitehead. 1980. Preliminary geology and paleontology of the Bodo D'ar hominid site, Afar, Ethiopia. *Palaeogeog., Palaeoclim., Palaeoecol.* 30: 107–120.

Kent, P. 1941. The recent history and Pleistocene deposits of the plateau north of Lake Eyasi, Tanganyika. *Geol. Mag.* (London) 78: 173–184.

Kunz, K., H. Kreuzer, and P. Müller. 1975. Potassium-Argon age determinations of the Trap Basalt of the southeastern part of the Afar rift. In *Afar Depression of Ethiopia*, eds. A. Pilger and A. Rösler, 370–374. Stuttgart: E. Schweizerbart'sche Verlag.

Larson, P., Jr. 1977. Matabaietu: An Oldowan site from the Afar, Ethiopia. *Nyame Akuma* 11: 6–10.

Laws, R. M. 1966. Age criteria for the African elephant. *E. Afr. Wildlife Jour.* 4: 1–14.

Leakey, M. D. 1975. Cultural patterns in the Olduvai sequence. In *After the Australopithecines: Stratigraphy, Ecology, and Cultural Change in the Middle Pleistocene*, eds. K. W. Butzer and G. L. Isaac, 477–493. The Hague: Mouton Publishers.

———. 1978. Olduvai fossil hominids: Their stratigraphic positions and associations. In *Early Hominids of Africa*, ed. C. J. Jolly, 3–16. New York: St. Martin's Press.

Lewin, R. 1983. Ethiopia halts prehistory research. *Science* 219: 147–149.

Linnaeus, C. 1758. *Systema naturae per regina tria naturae, secundum classes, ordines, genera, species cum characteribus, differentus; synonymis, locis.* Edito decima, refommata, I. Laurenti Slavii, Holmiae.

McDougall, I., T. Davies, R. Maier, and R. Rudowsi. 1985. Age of the Okote Tuff Complex, Koobi Fora, northern Kenya. *Nature* 316: 792–794.

MacInnes, D. G. 1942. Miocene and post-Miocene Proboscidea from East Africa. *Trans. Zool. Soc. London* 25: 33–106.

Maglio, V. J. 1969. The status of the East African elephant 'Archidiskodon exoptatus' Dietrich 1942. *Breviora* 336: 1–25.

———. 1970a. Four new species of Elephantidae from the Plio-Pleistocene of northwestern Kenya. *Breviora* 341: 1–43.

———. 1970b. Early Elephantidae of Africa and a tentative correlation of African Plio-Pleistocene deposits. *Nature* 225: 328–332.

———. 1972. Evolution of mastication in the Elephantidae. *Evolution* 26(4): 638–658.

———. 1973. Origin and evolution of the Elephantidae. *Amer. Phil. Soc. Trans.* 63(3): 1–149.

Maglio, V. J., and Q. B. Hendey. 1970. New evidence relating to the supposed stegolophodont ancestry of the Elephantidae. *S. Afr. Arch. Bull.* 35(3–4): 85–87.

Maglio, V. J., and A. B. Ricca. 1977. Dental and skeletal morphology of the earliest
    elephants. *Verhand. Koninklijke Nederl. Sakad. Wetenschappen, Afd. Natuurkunde
    Eerste Reeks* 29: 1-51.
Makinouchi, T., T. Koyaguchi, T. Matsuda, H. Mitsushio, and A. Ishida. 1984.
    Geology of the Nachola area and the Samburu Hills, west of Baragoi,
    Northern Kenya. *Afr. Study Monographs* (Kyoto University) 2: 15-44.
Marshall, E. 1987. Gossip and peer review at NSF. *Science* 238: 1502.
Matsuda, T., M. Torii, T. Koyaguchi, T. Makinouchi, H. Mitsushio, and S. Ishida.
    1984. Fission-track, K-Ar age determinations and palaeo-magnetic measure-
    ments of Miocene volcanic rocks in the western area of Baragoi, northern
    Kenya: Age of hominids. *Afr. Study Monographs* (Kyoto University) 2: 57-66.
Mebrate, A. 1976. A primitive fossil elephant molar from northwest Hararghe.
    Rift Valley Research Mission in Ethiopia. Report to the Ethiopian Ministry of
    Culture (Addis Ababa) No. 5: 1-16.
————. 1977. Fossil Proboscidea from the Middle Awash Valley. Rift Valley
    Research Mission in Ethiopia. Report to the Ethiopian Ministry of Culture
    (Addis Ababa) No. 9: 1-15.
————. 1983. Late Miocene-middle Pleistocene proboscidean fossil remains from
    the Middle Awash Valley, Afar Depression, Ethiopia. M.Sc. thesis, Univ. of
    Kansas, Lawrence.
Mebrate, A., and J. Kalb. 1981. A primitive elephantid from the Middle Awash
    Valley, Afar Depression, Ethiopia. *Sinet: Ethiopian Jour. Sci.* 4(1): 45-55.
————. 1985. Anancinae (Proboscidea: Gomphotheriidae) from the Middle
    Awash Valley, Afar, Ethiopia. *Jour. Vert. Paleont.* 5: 93-102.
Nakaya, H., M. Pickford, Y. Nakano, and H. Ishida. 1984. The late Miocene large
    mammal fauna from the Namurungule Formation, Samburu Hills, northern
    Kenya. *Afr. Study Monographs* (Kyoto University) 2: 87-132.
Nesbitt, L. M. 1935. *Desert and Forest*. Oxford: Alden Press.
Osborn, H. F. 1918. A long-jawed mastodon skeleton from South Dakota and
    phylogeny of the Proboscidea. *Bull. Geol. Soc. Amer.* 29: 133-137.
————. 1921. Evolution, phylogeny and classification of the Mastodontoidea.
    Bull. Geol. Soc. Amer. 32: 327-332.
————. 1928. Mammoths and man in the Transvaal. *Nature* 71: 672-673.
————. 1936. *Proboscidea*. Vol. 1. New York: American Museum Press.
————. 1942. *Proboscidea*. Vol. 2. New York: American Museum Press.
Partridge, T. C. 1973. Geomorphological dating of cave openings at Makapansgat,
    Sterkfontein, Swartkrans and Tauna. *Nature* 246: 75-79.
————. 1978. Re-appraisal of lithostratigraphy of Sterkfontein hominid site.
    Nature 275: 282-287.
————. 1979. Re-appraisal of lithostratigraphy of Makapansgat limeworks hom-
    inid site. *Nature* 279: 484-488.
Patterson, B., A. K. Behrensmeyer, and W. D. Sill. 1970. Geology and fauna of
    a new Pliocene locality in northwestern Kenya. *Nature* 276: 918-921.
Petrocchi, C. 1941. Il giacimento fossilifero di Sahabi. *Boll. Soc. Geol. Ital.* 50:
    107-114.
————. 1943. Il giacimento fossilifero di Sahabi. Parte 2, Paleontologia. *Colliezione
    Scientifica e Documentaria dell'Africa Italian, Ministero dell'Africa Italiana* 12:
    69-167.
————. 1954. Paleontologia di Sahabi. Parte I. Proboscidati di Sahabi. *Rend.
    Accad. Naz. (Roma)*, ser. 4, 4-5: 8-74.
Pickford, M. 1986. Cainozoic paleontological sites of western Kenya. *Münchner
    geowiss. Abh.* 8: 1-151.

————. 1987. The geology and palaeontology of the Kanam erosion gullies (Kenya). *Mainzer geowiss. Mitt.* 16: 209–226.

Pickford, M., H. Nakaya, H. Ishida, and Y. Nakano. 1984. The biostratigraphic analyses of the faunas of the Nachola area and Samburu Hills, northern Kenya. *Afr. Study Monograph* (Kyoto University) 2: 67–72.

Pickford, M., B. Senut, G. Poupeau, F. H. Brown, and B. Haileab. 1991. Correlation of tephra layers from the Western Rift Valley (Uganda) to the Turkana Basin (Ethiopia/Kenya) and the Gulf of Aden. *C. R. Acad. Sci., Paris* 313(2): 223–229.

Pickford, M., B. Senut, H. Roche, P. Mein, G. Ndaati, P. Obwona, and J. Tuhumwire. 1989. Uganda Paleontology Expedition: Résultats de la deuxième mission (1987) dans la région de Kisegi-Nyabusosi (bassin du lac Albert, Ouganda. *C. R. Acad. Sci., Paris* 308(2): 1751–1758.

Pickford, M., B. Senut, I. Ssemmanda, D. Elepu, and P. Obwona. 1988. Premiers résultats de la mission de l'Uganda Paleontology Expedition à Nkondo (Pliocène du Bassin du Lac Albert, Ouganda). *C. R. Acad. Sci., Paris* 306(2): 315–320.

Pilger, A., and A. Rösler, eds. 1975. *Afar Depression of Ethiopia.* Stuttgart: E. Schweizerbart'sche Verlag.

Plummer, T. W., and R. Potts. 1989. Excavations and new findings at Kanjera, Kenya. *Jour. Human Evol.* 18: 269–276.

Pomel, A. 1879. Ossements d'Éléphants et d'Hippopotames découvertes dans une station préhistorique de la plaine d'Eghis (Province d'Oran). *Bull. Soc. géol. France,* ser. 3, 7: 44–51.

————. 1895. Les éléphants Quaternaires de l'Algérie. *Paléontologie Monographies* No. 6.

Powers, D. W. 1980. Geology of Mio-Pliocene sediments of the lower Kerio River Valley, Kenya. Ph.D. diss., Princeton University, New Jersey.

Roche, H., and J-J. Tiercelin. 1980. Industries lithiques de la formation Plio-Pléistocène d'Hadar Éthiopie (campagne 1976). In *Proceedings of the 8th Panafrican Congress of Prehistory and Quaternary Studies Nairobi (September 1977),* eds. R. E. Leakey and B. A. Ogott, 194–199. Nairobi: Intern. Louis Leakey Memorial Inst. for African Prehistory.

Roth, V. L. 1989. Fabricational noise in elephant dentition. *Paleobiology* 15: 165–179.

Saegusa, H. 1987. Cranial morphology and phylogeny of the stegodonts. *Compass* 64: 221–243.

Sanders, W. J. 1990. Fossil Proboscidea from the Pliocene Lusso Beds of the Western Rift, Zaire. *Virginia Mus. Nat. Hist. Mem.* 1: 171–187.

Sarwar, M. 1977. Taxonomy and distribution of the Siwalik Proboscidea. *Bull. Department Zoology* (University of Punjab, Lahore) 10: 1–172.

Schmitt, T. J., and A. E. Nairn. 1984. Interpretation of the magnetostratigraphy of the Hadar hominid site, Ethiopia. *Nature* 309: 704–706.

Shipman, P., A. Walker, J. A. Van Couvering, P. J. Hooker, and J. A. Miller. 1981. Fort Ternan hominoid site, Kenya: Geology, age, taphonomy and palaeoecology. *Jour. Human Evol.* 10: 49–72.

Sickenberg, O., and M. Schönfeld. 1975. The Chorora Formation — lower Pliocene limnical sediments in the southern Afar (Ethiopia). In *Afar Depression of Ethiopia,* eds. A. Pilger and A. Rösler, 277–284. Stuttgart: E. Schweizerbart'sche Verlag.

Sikes, S. K. 1971. *The Natural History of the African Elephant.* London: Weidenfeld and Nicolsen.

Simons, E. L., and E. Delson. 1978. Cercopithecidae and Parapithecidae. In *Evo-*

lution of African Mammals, eds. V. J. Maglio and H. B. S. Cooke, 100–119. Cambridge: Harvard Univ. Press.

Simpson, G. G. 1945. The principles of classification and a classification of mammals. *Amer. Mus. Nat. Hist. Bull.* 85: 1–350.

Smart, C. 1976. The Lothagam 1 fauna: Its phylogenetic, ecological, and biogeographic significance. In *Earliest Man and Environments in the Lake Rudolf Basin*, eds. Y. Coppens, F. C. Howell, G. L. Isaac, and R. Leakey, 361–369. Chicago: Univ. of Chicago Press.

Stanley, D. J., and F.-C. Wezel, eds. 1985. *Geological Evolution of the Mediterranean Basin*. New York: Springer Verlag.

Swofford, D. L. 1989. *PAUP—Phylogenetic Analysis Using Parsimony, Version 3.0A.* Champaign: Illinois Natural History Survey.

Swofford, D. L., and G. J. Olsen. 1990. Phylogeny reconstruction. In *Molecular Systematics*, eds. D. M. Hillis and C. Moritz, 411–490. Sunderland, Mass.: Sinauer Associates.

Taieb, M. 1974. Évolution Quaternaire du bassin de l'Awash. Ph.DS. diss., l'Univ. Paris VI.

Taieb, M., Y. Coppens, D. C. Johanson, and J. E. Kalb. 1972. Dépôts sédimentaires et faunes du Plio-Pléistocène de la basse vallée de l'Awash (Afar central, Éthiopie). *C. R. Acad. Sci., Paris* 275: 819–822.

Taieb, M., Y. Coppens, D. C. Johanson, and J. L. Aronson. 1976. Geological and palaeontological background of Hadar hominid site, Afar, Ethiopia. *Nature* 260: 289–293.

Taieb, M., D. C. Johanson, Y. Coppens, R. Bonnefille, and J. E. Kalb. 1974. Découverte d'hominides dans les séries Plio-Pléistocènes d'Hadar (Bassin de l'Awash; Afar, Éthiopie). *C. R. Acad. Sci., Paris* 279: 735–738.

Taieb, M., D. C. Johanson, Y. Coppens, and J.-J. Tiercelin. 1978. Expedition internationale de l'Afar, Ethiopie (4e et 5e campagnes 1975–1977: Chronostratigraphie des gisements a hominides Pliocènes d'Hadar et corrélations avec les sites préhistorique du Kada Gona. *C. R. Acad. Sci., Paris* 279: 735–738.

Taruno, H. 1985. Genus *Stegodon* and genus *Stegolophodon*. *Bull. Osaka Mus. Nat. Hist.* 38: 23–36.

Tassy, P. 1983. Les Elephantoidea Miocènes du Plateau du Potwar, Groupe de Siwalik, Pakistan. *Ann. Paléontol.* 69: 99–136, 235–298, 317–354.

———. 1986. *Nouveaux Elephantoidea (Mammalia) dans le Miocène du Kenya.* Cahiers de Paléontologie Est-africaine. Paris: Éditions Centre National de la Recherche Scientifique.

———. 1988. The classification of Proboscidea: How many cladistic classifications? *Cladistics* 4: 43–57.

———. 1990. Phylogénie et classification des Proboscidea (Mammalia): Historique et actualité. *Ann. Paléont.* 76: 159–224.

Tassy, P., and P. Darlu. 1986. Analyse cladistique numérique et analyse de parcimonie; l'exemple des Elephantidae. *Geobios* 19: 587–600.

Tassy, P., and J. Shoshani. 1988. The Tethytheria: Elephants and their relatives. In Vol. 2, *The Phylogeny and Classification of the Tetrapods*, ed. M. J. Benton, 283–315. Special Volume 35B. Oxford: Systematics Assoc.

Thesiger, W. 1935. The Awash River and the Ausa sultanate. *Geogr. Jour., London* 85: 1–19.

Tiercelin, J.-J., J. Michaux, and Y. Bandet. 1979. Le Miocène supérieur du sud de la Dépression de l'Afar, Éthiopie: Sédiments, faunes, âges isotopiques. *Bull. Soci. géol. France* 21(3): 255–258.

Tobias, P. V. 1980. A survey and synthesis of the African hominids of the late Tertiary and early Quaternary periods. In *Current Arguments on Early Man*, ed.
L. K. Konigsson, 86–113. Oxford: Clarendon Press.

Tobien, H. 1973. The structure of the mastodont molar (Proboscidea Mammalia).
Part 1: The bunodont pattern. *Mainzer geowiss. Mitt* 2: 115–147.

———. 1978. On the evolution of mastodonts (Proboscidea, Mammalia). Part 2:
The bunodont tetralophodont group. *Geol. Jb. Hessen* 106: 159–208.

Tobien, H., G. Chen, and Y. Li. 1988. Mastodonts (Proboscidea, Mammalia) from
the late Neogene and early Pleistocene of the People's Republic of China.
Mainzer Geowiss. 17: 95–220.

United Nations Geothermal Project. 1973. Investigation of geothermal resources
for power development. United Nations Development Programme (New
York), Technical Report: 1–175.

Vacek, M. 1877. Über österreiche Mastodonten und ihre Beziehungen zu den Mas-
todonarten Europas. *Abh. geol. Reichsanst.* 7(4): 1–45.

Van Zinderen Bakker, E. M., and J. H. Mercer. 1986. Major late Cainozoic climatic
events and palaeoenvironmental changes in Africa viewed in a world wide
context. *Palaeogeog., Palaeoclim., Palaeoecol.* 56: 217–235.

Varet, J. 1978. *Geology of Central and Southern Afar (Ethiopia and Djibouti Republic).*
Paris: Centre National de la Recherche Scientifique.

Verniers, J., and J. deHeinzelin. 1990. Stratigraphy and geological history of the
upper Semliki: A preliminary report. *Virginia Mus. Nat. Hist. Mem.* 1: 17–39.

Vrba, E. S. 1975. Some evidence of chronology and palaeoecology of Sterkfontein, Swartkrans and Kromdraai from the fossil Bovidae. *Nature* 254: 301–304.

———. 1982. Biostratigraphy and chronology, based particularly on Bovidae, of
southern African hominid-associated assemblages. In Vol. 2, *Proceedings of
Congrès Internationale de Paléontologie Humaine*, eds. H. de Lumley and M. A. de
Lumley, 707–752. Nice: Union Internationale des Sciences Préhistoriques et
Protohistoriques.

———. 1988. Late Pliocene climatic events and hominid evolution. In *Evolutionary History of the "Robust" Australopithecines*, ed. F. E. Grine, 405–426. New
York: Aldine de Gruyter.

Walter, R. C. 1989. Application and limitation of fission-track geochronology to
Quaternary tephras. *Quat. Intern.* 1: 35–46.

Walter, R. C., and J. L. Aronson. 1982. Revisions of K/Ar Ages for the Hadar hominid site, Ethiopia. *Nature* 296: 122–127.

Walter, R. C., P. C. Manega, R. L. Hay, R. E. Drake, and G. H. Curtis. 1991. Laser-
fusion $^{40}Ar/^{39}Ar$ dating of Bed 1, Olduvai Gorge, Tanzania. *Nature* 354:
145–149.

Walter, R. C., J. A. Westgate, W. K. Hart, and J. L. Aronson. 1984. Tephrostratigraphic correlation of the Sidi Hakoma and Tulu Bor tuffs: Nd isotope and
new trace element data. *Geol. Soc. Amer., Abstract with Program* 16: 48497.

Walter, R. C., J. A. Westgate, G. Wolde-Gabriel, J. L. Aronson, and W. K. Hart.
1985a. Geochemical and temporal patterns of felsic volcanism in Ethiopia.
Geol. Soc. Amer., Abstract with Programs 17: 56006.

Walter, R. C., G. Wolde-Gabriel, and J. A. Westgate. 1985b. Correlation of ash
flow tuffs with distal air fall tephra: Significance for Pliocene tephrostratig-
raphy of hominid-bearing sediments in Ethiopia. *Geol. Soc. Amer. Abstract with
Programs* 17: 77875.

Westphal, M., J. Chavaillon, and J.-J. Jaeger. 1979. Magnétostratigraphie des
dépôts pléistocènes de Melka-Kunturé (Éthiopie): premières données. *Bull.
Soc. géol. France* 21(3): 227–232.

White, T. D., R. V. Moore, and G. Suwa. 1984. Hadar biostratigraphy and hominid evolution. *Jour. Vert. Paleont.* 4(4): 575–583.

Williams, M. A. J., G. Assefa, and D. A. Adamson. 1986. Depositional context
of Plio-Pleistocene hominid-bearing formations in the Middle Awash Valley,
southern Afar rift, Ethiopia. In *Sedimentation in the African Rifts*, eds. L. E. Frostick, R. W. Renaut, I. Reid, and J. J. Tiercelin, 241–251. Special Publication 25.
London: Geological Society.

Yabe, H. 1950. Three alleged occurrences of *Stegolophodon latidens* (Clift) in Japan.
Proc. Japan Acad. 26(9): 61–65.

Young, Chung-Chien. 1935. Miscellaneous mammalian fossils from Shani and
Honan. *Paleont. Sinica* 9(C): 1–57.

Zanettin, B., and E. Justin-Visentin. 1974. The volcanic succession in central Ethi-
opia. Part 2. The volcanics of the western Afar and Ethiopian rift margins.
Centro di Studio per la Geologia e la Petrologia della Formazioni Cristalline, 1–19.
Padova: Consiglio Nazionale delle Ricerche.

APPENDIX

Phylogenetic Systematics of Late Neogene
Afro-Eurasian Elephantoidea

The following summarizes the cladistic analysis of Kalb et al. (1992a) of late Neogene African and Eurasian Elephantoidea in order to place the Middle Awash *Anancus* and elephantid fossils into the phylogenetic model used in this report.

This study adopted the parsimony methods formulated by Hennig (1966) and expanded upon by Swofford and others (Swofford and Olsen 1990). Swofford's (1989, Version 3.0A) computer program, "Phylogenetic Analysis Using Parsimony" (PAUP), was employed using unordered, rooted, branch-and-bound search settings. Accelerated transformations (ACCTRAN) were relied upon for character-state optimization, which place equivocal character transformations *down* tree branches. Delayed transformations (DELTRAN) were also reported on, which place equivocal character transformations *up* tree branches. Detailed taxa and character descriptions used in this analysis are contained in Kalb et al. (1992a, Appendices I and II) and summarized in Table 1 in this appendix.

The PAUP analysis resulted in a singlemost parsimonious tree (Fig. 1) with 61 transformations and a consistency index of 0.689, based on 18 taxa and 34 characters. No autapomorphic characters were used in the analysis, nor were assumptions made in scoring the data matrix with regard to missing or incomplete data. Various tests were made to test the stability of the tree as described by Kalb et al. (1992a). In the analysis, three characters (32–34) are multistate, six (2, 8, 12, 16, 28, 32) show unequivocal convergence, and six (11, 13, 21, 22, 30, 31) show unequivocal reversals. Characters showing equivocation indicated by DELTRAN or ACCTRAN are distinguished in Fig. 2.

103

	Elephas	Mammuthus	Lox. adaurora	Loxodonta Group	Primelephas	Stegodon	Stegodibelodon	Stegol. orbus	Stegol. syrticus	Stegolophodon	A. Sagantole	A. petrocchii	A. Langebaanweg	A. "kenyensis"	Paratetralophodon	Tetralophodon	"M." grandincisivus	Phiomia
CRANIUM/MANDIBLE																		
1 Cranium: flattened (0), rounded (1).	1	1	1	1	9	1	9	9	1	9	9	9	9	1	1	1	0	0
2 Occipital condyles: protruding (0), recessed (1).	1	1	0	0	9	0	9	9	1	9	9	9	9	0	0	0	0	0
3 Basicranium: not erect (0), erect (1).	1	1	1	1	9	1	9	9	1	9	9	9	9	1	1	0	0	0
4 Cranium: non-globular (0), globular (1).	0	1	1	1	9	0	9	9	0	9	9	9	9	0	0	0	0	0
5 Fronto-parietal region: not concave (0), concave (1).	1	0	0	0	9	0	9	9	0	9	9	9	9	9	0	0	0	0
6 Mandible width: narrow (0), wide (1).	1	1	1	1	9	1	1	9	1	1	9	0	9	1	9	0	1	0
TUSKS/MANDIBULAR SYMPHYSIS																		
7 Premaxillary tusk sheaths: narrow (0), flaring (1).	0	1	1	9	9	0	9	9	9	9	9	9	9	9	0	0	9	0
8 Upper tusks: downturned (0), not downturned (1).	1	1	1	1	9	1	9	9	1	9	9	9	9	1	0	0	1	0
9 Upper tusks: not upturned (0), upturned (1).	1	1	1	1	1	1	9	9	1	9	9	9	9	0	0	0	0	0
10 Extended mandibular symphysis: not downturned (0), downturned(1).	9	9	9	9	9	9	1	1	1	1	9	9	9	9	1	1	0	0
11 Mandibular symphysis: extended (0), shortened or fully reduced (1).	1	1	1	1	9	1	1	0	0	1	9	1	9	1	0	0	0	0
12 Mandibular symphysis: extended or shortened (0), fully reduced (1)	1	1	1	1	9	0	0	0	0	0	9	9	9	1	0	0	0	0
13 Lower tusks: present (0), absent or vestigial (1).	1	1	1	1	9	1	1	0	0	1	9	1	9	1	0	0	0	0
14 Lower tusks: flat or pyriform (0), circular (1).	9	9	9	9	9	9	9	1	1	9	9	9	9	9	9	1	0	0
MOLARS																		
15 Curvilinear alignment of apices: absent (0), present (1).	1	1	1	1	1	1	1	1	1	1	0	0	0	0	0	0	0	0
16 Distinctly brachydont molars: absent (0), present (1).	0	0	0	0	0	1	0	0	0	1	0	0	0	0	0	0	0	0
17 Anancoidy: absent (0), present (1).	0	0	0	0	0	0	0	0	0	0	1	1	1	1	0	0	0	0
18 Posterior face of lophids or lower plates: very convex (0), shallow convex or absent (1).	1	1	1	1	1	1	1	1	1	1	0	0	0	0	0	0	0	0

Char.	Description	Data matrix (taxa →)
19	Posterior face of lophids or lower plates: not concave (0), shallow concave or very concave (1).	1 1 1 1 1 0 0 0 0 1 0 0 0 0 0 0 0 0 0
20	Posterior face of lophids or lower plates: convex or mixed (0), concave (1)	1 1 1 1 1 0 0 0 0 0 0 0 0 0 0 0 0 0 0
21	Anterior face of lophids or lower plates: convex (0), concave or mixed (1).	1 0 1 1 1 1 0 0 0 1 0 0 0 0 0 0 0 0 0
22	Anterior face of lophids or lower plates: convex or mixed (0), concave (1).	1 0 1 1 1 0 0 0 0 0 0 0 0 0 0 0 0 0 0
23	Plates: absent (0), present (1).	1 1 1 1 1 1 0 1 1 1 0 1 1 0 0 0 0 0 0
24	Loph(id)s/plates: expanded (0), distinctly compressed (1).	1 1 1 1 1 0 0 1 1 1 0 0 0 1 0 0 0 0 0

MOLAR ACCESSORIES

Char.	Description	Data matrix (taxa →)
25	Median sulcus: present (0), absent (1).	1 1 1 1 1 0 0 0 0 1 0 0 0 0 0 0 0 0 0
26	Median sulcus: complete (0), incomplete (1).	9 9 9 9 9 1 1 1 1 9 0 1 0 1 0 0 0 0 0
27	Four apices (cones, conelets): present (0), five or more (1).	1 1 1 1 1 0 0 1 1 1 0 0 0 1 0 0 0 0 0
28	On M_2-M_3, posterior posttrite conules/columns: anteriorly (0), posteriorly (1).	0 0 1 0 0 0 0 0 0 0 0 0 0 0 0 0 0 0 0
29	On M^2-M^3 with lophs, three posterior posttrite conules: absent (0), present (1).	9 9 9 9 9 9 9 9 9 9 0 9 9 9 0 0 0 0 0
30	On M_2 and M_3, posterior pretrite conules/columns posteriorly: present (0), reduced/fused (1).	0 1 1 1 1 0 1 1 1 1 0 0 1 1 0 0 0 0 0
31	On M^3, posterior pretrite conules/columns posteriorly: absent (0), present (1).	9 1 1 9 9 9 9 1 1 9 1 1 1 1 1 1 1 1 0

LOPH(ID)/PLATE NUMBER

Char.	Description	Data matrix (taxa →)
32	On M_2 or M^2, minimum of: three (0), four (1), five (2), six (3).	2 3 9 3 3 1 2 2 9 3 1 2 9 3 1 1 2 2 0
33	On M_3, minimum of: three (0), five (1), six (2), seven (3), eight (4).	4 4 4 4 3 2 3 3 3 3 2 3 3 3 1 2 2 2 0
34	On M^3, minimum of: three (0), five (1), six (2), seven (3), nine (4).	3 4 4 4 3 1 1 1 1 3 1 1 1 3 1 2 3 3 0

APPENDIX TABLE 1. Data matrix for the cladogram in Figures 1 and 2 of this appendix.

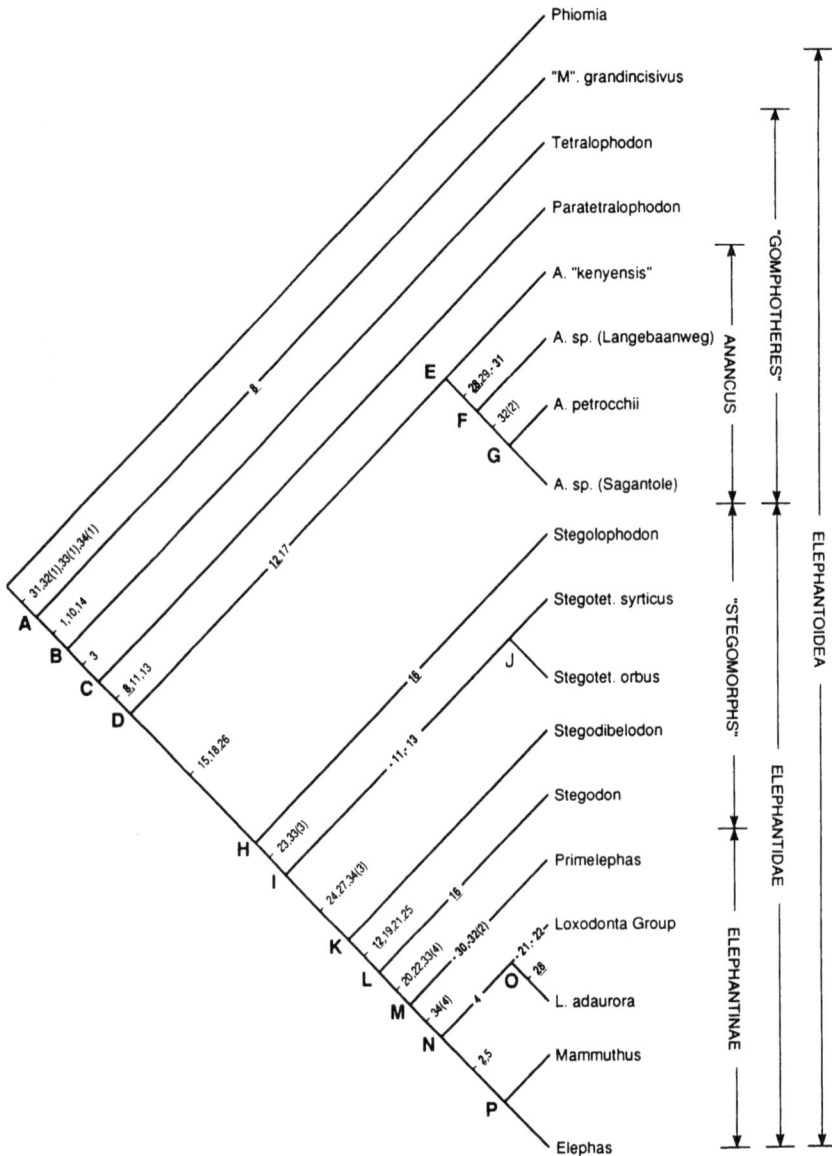

APPENDIX FIGURE 1.　Cladogram of late Neogene Proboscidea.

APPENDIX FIGURE 2. Cladogram with equivocal characters from Appendix Figure 1.

GEOGRAPHICAL AND
STRATIGRAPHICAL NAME INDEX

TAXA INDEX

AUTHOR INDEX*

* Senior author entries only of multiple author citations.

113

www.ingramcontent.com/pod-product-compliance
Lightning Source LLC
Chambersburg PA
CBHW061755260326
41914CB00006B/1122